I0434892

# Learn to Drive

## Obtain Your Licence in Nine Easy Steps

Geoffrey Shakumbila

ISBN 10: 1494957469
ISBN-13: 978-1494957469

# PREFACE

The aim of Learn to Drive text

This book has been written for learner drivers. It prepares learner-drivers for theory as well as practical tests. Each lesson starts by referring you to the appropriate rules in the Highway Code. By studying all the chapters systematically, you will have gone through almost all of the Highway Code rules at the end of the course. This guide includes lessons for vehicles with manual as well as an automatic transmission system.

You should study the book in the sequence of the chapters so that you can gradually increase your knowledge and skills. Even though you may find that certain topics are familiar than others, you should, by all means, attempt to do every exercise and spend a little more time on topics you find difficult to practice.

In this modern world, the need to drive competently is increasingly becoming more necessary than ever. As the number of drivers increase, government agencies are making frantic efforts to bring awareness of the dangers of incompetent driving. Therefore, right from the beginning, it is important to grasp these important basic skills and rules.

Learner drivers can study his book in conjunction with the Highway Code. Driving instructors and qualified drivers, too, can use this book for reference.

# Table of Contents

I am indeed grateful to the following individuals and organisations for permission to reproduce photographs and other copyright materials:

- Zambian Highway Code, fifth edition, by Ministry of Communications and Transport (Zambia)
- Department for Transport (United Kingdom), Office of Public Sector Information (United Kingdom)
- Excerpts from LEARN TO DRIVE IN TEN EASY STEPS by Nigel Stacey, Margaret Stacey and Andrew Rice, copyright 1987, published by Kogan Page, U.K.

shaksjeff@yahoo.com
jeffshaks@gmail.com

# 1 INTRODUCTION

The lessons in this book are practical to ensure learner drivers acquire the desired knowledge and develop necessary skills by the time they complete this course. They have been arranged in a logical sequence so that you follow them step-by-step without skipping any. To practice on the road, you will require a qualified driver or an approved instructor to guide you. If you have a family car, your instructor can be a friend, relative, or a hired person. However, you must ensure that the person instructing you has a minimum of three years continuous driving experience and is able to take you through the lessons thoroughly.

| Icon key | |
|---|---|
| | Tip |
| | Warning |
| | Incorrect |
| | Correct |

Find a good instructor who has the necessary experience and ability. With the help of this book, he or she will guide you until you are able to drive safely on your own. While driving under supervision, make good use of the time and ask as many questions as you can to clear any doubts. You must gain extensive driving experience in a wide range of situations such as driving at night and in wet weather. When you have covered all the lessons and gained the experience on the road, you will be confident to attempt your driving test.

Make sure you understand a particular subject before you go out to practice. Read the subject carefully and thoroughly, noting down the important points. These are the points your instructor will repeat to you, so knowing them in advance helps.

Although most people prefer using a football field for learning purposes, you can start on a residential road or street that is not busy. After a few sessions, you will be confident to move to the busier roads where you can drive at fairly higher speeds.

Another important book you must have on hand is a Highway Code. Get a copy.

You will be referring to it mostly at the beginning of each chapter.

## Rules for Drivers

Once you obtain your driver's licence, you will be held accountable to the traffic rules and regulations concerning driving on public roads. For this reason, you will do everything to your ability to ensure the safety of others and yourself. Besides following the rules and regulations, you should act responsibly, at the same time respecting other road users.

## Do not drink and drive

A leading problem with many drivers is alcohol intake that results in fatal traffic accidents. Alcohol causes someone to start reacting slowly to situations, and he fails to coordinate effectively with his eyes, feet and hands. It also impairs his vision and blurs his judgement about the speed of traffic. Just a little amount of alcohol leaves him in a state he cannot tell how fast he is travelling or tell accurately the distance between him and other road users. With such poor judgement, he cannot respond correctly.

According to United Nations Education, Scientific and Cultural Organisation (UNESCO) calculations in its module 23, you can determine in general terms the alcohol content in your body. If a 375ml bottle of beer has 5 per cent alcohol content, this means the volume of alcohol is 18.75ml. Taking four bottles will result in having 75ml of the volume of alcohol in your body. When you are immediately tested, the result of alcohol content in the blood will be 30 micrograms or a reading of 0.30 on the breathalyser, enough to be penalised by a traffic officer. But this does not mean that someone is drunk.

Alcohol content has nothing to do with someone getting drunk but more to do with losing the ability to coordinate well and to make good judgement when on the wheel. If you are driving, irrespective of the distance you will travel, stay away from the bottle.

## Drugs

Certain drugs and medicines also give you similar reactions as alcohol does. Some can cause drowsiness, nausea, hallucination, or even make someone fall asleep. Doctors normally recommend that patients taking medication that may cause drowsiness should not operate machines or drive.

As concentration is vital, you must be in the right state of mind when driving. A headache, stomachache or other ailments may bring about discomfort and cause you to respond inappropriately. If you are taking any prescribed medication from a health practitioner, seek advice on whether you can drive or not.

## Tiredness

You should not drive when tired to avoid the risk of colliding with other road users. Before you begin a journey, make sure your mind is fresh and you are fit. Always plan your journey by taking into account the time you will depart and the distance to be covered. Then determine the speed to maintain to estimate the time of arrival. If you are travelling in the morning, do not drink. Go to bed early to get enough rest. During a long trip, stop at convenient places for short breaks of at least 15 minutes.

Unplanned journeys usually involve unnecessary and risky speeding. Because you are behind schedule, you are forced to drive fast so that you can recover the lost time. Travelling at night between midnight and 6 a.m. is not advisable as the state of mind during this period is less alert.

## Before Setting off

Plan the route you will be taking and give yourself sufficient time. On the way, you will avoid congested routes and making unexpected turns.

In addition, consider the temperature, type of footwear and clothing. High-heeled shoes and tight-fitting clothes can prevent you from using the controls properly. In hot weather, open the windows to allow plenty of fresh air. During the cold weather, you can turn on the heater to keep warm, but do not raise the temperature too high.

Always wear your seatbelt even if you are travelling for a short distance. If you have passengers with you, remind them to buckle their seatbelts. If a child less than 3 years of age has to occupy a seat, have a correct child restraint installed.

## Dashboard

It is best not to place any items, such as books and drinks, on the dashboard. While you are driving, they can fall under the pedals and prevent you from applying the brakes, for instance. In addition, when you apply emergency brakes, small items on the dashboard could turn into dangerous missiles and cause serious injuries to you or your passengers.

# 2 CAR PROFILE

Before you can drive away, first look at the various controls and carry out some exercises while the vehicle is stationary.

Study the following rules in the Highway Code before you proceed with the chapter:

| Rule No. | Rule | |
|---|---|---|
| 84, 85, 92, 93 | Seat belts and use of mirrors | |
| 112 | Neutral Gear. | |
| 196, 197, 243 | Use of horns | |
| 200 | Opening doors | |
| 190, 192, 193, 195, 241 - 242 | Use of headlights and hazard lights | |
| 234 - 240 | Giving and responding to signals | |

## 1.0 Internal and External Walkthrough

### 1.1 Doors

Before opening a car door, make sure you are safe. In parallel parking, use exterior mirrors to look out for approaching vehicles or cyclists (figure 2.1). Locking all the doors using central locking system is another measure you can take to prevent passengers from opening the doors until you have confirmed it is safe. Then, as quickly as possible, close them.

Figure 2.1 – Look behind before opening the door.

And just before driving off, confirm that all the doors are securely closed by looking at the door warning light in the instrument panel. If it is lit, then one of the doors is not properly closed. While the car is in motion, a door that is not properly closed will rattle, and can suddenly swing wide open to the detriment of yourself and other road users.

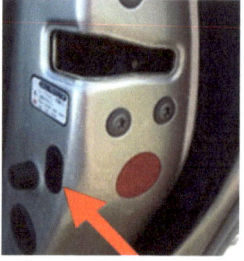

Figure 2.2 – Child-lock.

Child-locks, fitted on the rear doors, are additional safety measures to prevent children from opening them. They can only be opened from outside by yourself or another adult once the vehicle is stationary. To use a child-lock, open the door and locate it in the area shown in figure 2.2.

## 1.2 Seats

Front seats are fitted with knobs or levers to adjust position, backrest and height to correct and comfortable positions. After the necessary adjustments, you should reach the pedals without stretching yourself.

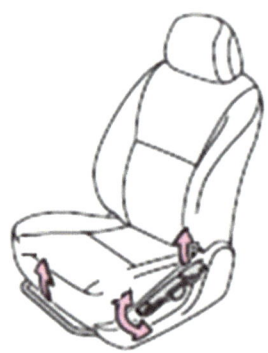

Figure 2.3 – Adjusting levers.

Figure 2.4 – Proper sitting posture.

The head restraint is another important safety device fitted on top of the backrest. In case of an accident, it reduces the risk of spine injuries and stops your neck from snapping back. It should be level with your eyes or ears as shown in figure 2.4.

## 1.3 Seatbelts

You and your passengers must always buckle your seatbelts every time you are on the road. However, these are unsuitable for young children below the age of three. If you are carrying a child, install a child restraint in the rear seat. See figure 2.5. Where this is not available, an adult can hold the child on the laps while occupying the rear seat.

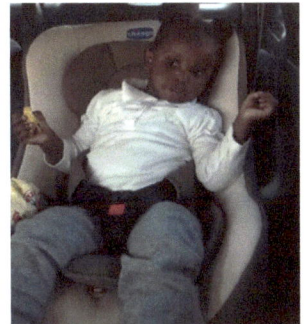

Figure 2.5 - Use a child restraint to secure your child.

No child should be allowed to stand between the two front seats. Otherwise, you expose him or her to great danger. In case of a head-on collision, even if you are driving at 30 Km/h, the child will be thrown onto the windscreen and out of the vehicle.

## 1.3   Steering Wheel

The most secure way of holding a steering wheel is to place both hands at 0900 hours and 1500 hours as shown in figure 2.6. You can also place them at 10.00 and 14.00 hours. You should hold the steering wheel with both hands most of the time.

Figure 2.6 - Hold the steering wheel with both hands.

To get familiar with the steering wheel, hold it loosely and allow your palms to slip around the rim. Relax your shoulders and keep your arms away from your body.

To give a signal for the right or left turn, push the lever up or down with your middle finger. It is more comfortable and safer than to take your hand off in order to push the lever. However, this is only possible when you have not set the headlamps on high beam.

Certain vehicles have a lever for adjusting the angle of a steering wheel. This lever is found on the steering column just below the steering wheel. To unlock the steering wheel, release the lever and adjust it to the desired position. Then push it back to lock the wheel.

## 1.4   Mirrors

Always use mirrors before you signal. When you intend to turn or change to an adjacent lane, check through the exterior and rear-view mirrors. However, you ought to be aware of a blind spot. At a certain point, vehicles that are about to overtake you cannot be seen in exterior mirrors. If you do not double-check, you are likely to enter the path of another vehicle and cause an accident. Figure 2.7 shows a motorbike that cannot be seen by a driver because it is in a blind spot.

To prevent an accident, check the blind spot by turning your head and glancing over your right or left shoulder. Do this to confirm the road is safe whenever you are pulling away or changing position.

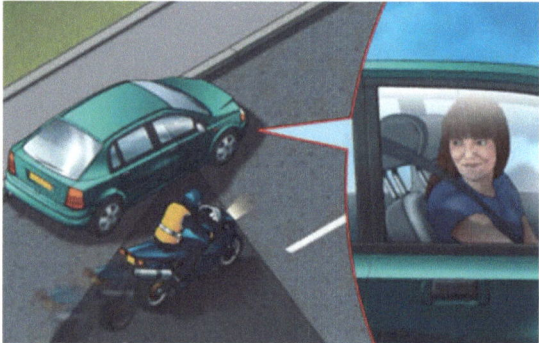

Figure 2.7 – Check your blind spot.

 One of the causes of road traffic accidents is failure to double –check before one changes to another lane.

## 1.5   Handbrake

The handbrake locks the rear wheels to keep the vehicle stationary. You should apply it only when you have come to a complete stop.  And a warning light in the dashboard glows red while the engine is running. Before you set the vehicle in motion, make you release it completely. This will turn off the light.

## 1.6   Gears

Cars have either a four or a five-speed gearbox. The gears 1 to 4 form an "H" appearance on the gear knob. Neutral is the middle position as shown in Figure 2.8. You engage the first four gears in exactly the same way on most car models. However, the reverse and 5th gears may be placed opposite to what is shown here.

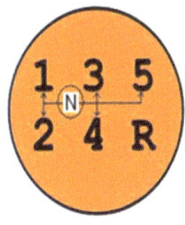

Figure 2.8 – Five Gear knob.

The extra 5th gear (or overdrive gear), is used normally outside the city limits where you can drive at speeds above 60 km/h. Once in the 5th gear, the engine speed reduces while the car moves faster. It also consumes less fuel and produces less noise. However, when you are driving above 100 km/h, fuel consumption increases.

## 1.7   How to Engage Gears

If you are practising on a vehicle with an automatic transmission, go to section 2.0 on page 11.

---

**Practice 1 – Engaging 1st and 2nd Gear from Neutral**

a).  While the handbrake is on, press the clutch all the way down.
b).  Hold the gear lever so that your palm is facing away from you as shown in Figure 2.9.
c).  Next, push the lever to the left as far as it can go, see Figure 2.10.
d).  Then push forward to engage 1st gear.
e).  While you are still pressing down the clutch, pull the lever straight back into 2nd gear.
f).  Release the clutch and relax your foot.

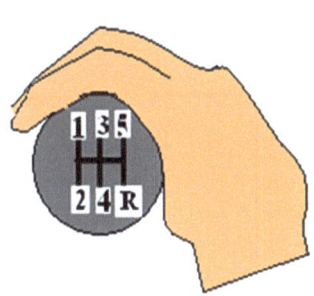

Figure 2.9 – Palm facing away.

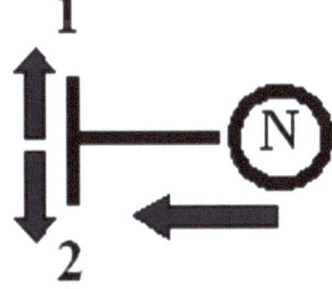

Figure 2.10 – Push to the left.

You may find it a bit hard at first. It rarely works the first time. However, more practice is what you need. An examiner expects you to select and engage the correct gear at the right time.

---

**Practice 2 – Engaging 3rd and 4th Gears from 2nd**

    a).   Press the clutch all the way down.
    b).   Hold the gear so your thumb is touching the head of the lever as shown in Figure 2.11.
    c).   Push straightforward, and then to the right through neutral and push forward into 3rd gear, see Figure 2.12.
    d).   While the clutch is pressed down, pull straight back into 4th.
    e).   Release the clutch and rest your foot.

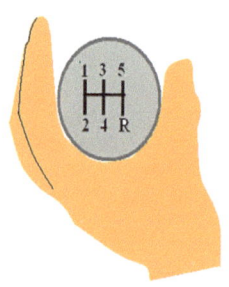

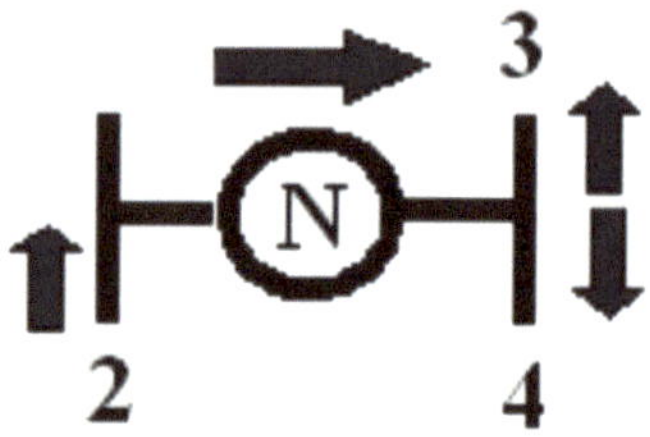

Figure 2.12 – Engage gear 3 and 4.

Figure 2.11 – Forefinger and thumb touching gear knob.

---

**Practice 3 – Engaging 5th Gear from 4th**

    a).   Press the clutch all the way down.
    b).   Hold the gear so your thumb is touching the head of the lever.
    c).   Push straight forward to neutral, then all the way to the right and forward into 5th gear.
    d).   Release the clutch and rest your foot.

To return to neutral, repeat step (a) and pull the lever into the central position. Repeat practice 1 to 3 until you are fully conversant.

---

**Practice 4 – Changing Down through the Gears**

Once you have gained as much experience as necessary with the above exercises, proceed to practise changing from high to low gears. Attempt changing the gears from high to low as follows:

- From 5th to 4th
- From 4th to 3rd
- From 3rd to 2nd

- From 2nd to 1st

Each time you are changing the gears, remember to press the clutch all the way down. Have enough time to practice again the above exercises until you are familiar.

## 1.8   Block Gear Selection

Alternatively, you can select gears in blocks. This is known as block gear selection. When changing down, it is not necessary to change gears in sequence. For example, after reducing the speed and you are going slowly enough, you can change from 4/5 to 2. You can also change from 4th to 2nd gear when the car has slowed down and is moving at between 20 and 30 km/h. Further, you can change from 3rd to 1st gear when the car is about to stop or is moving very slowly.

---

**Practice 5 – Engaging Reverse Gear**

a). Start by pressing the clutch down.
b). Hold the gear lever with your thumb touching the knob.
c). Push it to the right as far as it can go and pull straight down.

## 2.0 Automatic Transmission Walkthrough

An automatic transmission gearbox has no clutch. An accelerator and are used to increase the speed while the brake control reduces the speed and bring the vehicle to a complete stop. Furthermore, other models that do not have a handbrake have an additional pedal to the far left. This is used to lock or release the rear wheels.

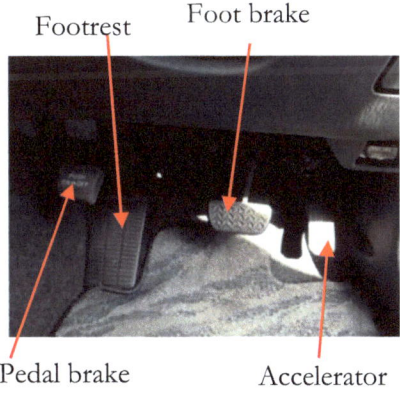

Fig.2.13— Automatic transmission pedals.

When the engine is running, the gear that you select is displayed in the instrument panel. This means you do not have to look down at the lever, especially at night. Note that the number of gears will vary from one car model to another.

## 2.1 Automatic Gear Selection Exercises

For this practice, the vehicle should be stationary and the engine switched off. Also, ensure that you have applied the handbrake. Insert the key in the ignition and turn it to "ACC". Note that you cannot engage any gear when the key is removed.

### Practice 1 – Engaging Drive Gear

To shift from park to drive gear:
  a)  Hold the gear selector and place your thumb over the gear selector lock button.
  b)  Press the footbrake down.
  c)  Then press and hold the button as you shift the gear to D.
  d)  Release the footbrake.

### Practice 2 – Engaging Reverse Gear

To shift from park to reverse gear:
  a). Hold the gear selector and place your thumb over the gear selector lock button.
  b). Press the footbrake down.
  c). Press and hold the button as you shift the gear selector to R.
  d). Release the footbrake

 You can only shift out of P gear when the footbrake is pressed.

# 3 STARTING OFF

This chapter shows you how to start the engine and drive away at steady and slow speeds. Study the following rules in the Highway Code before you proceed with this chapter:

| Rule No. | Rule |
|----------|------|
| 89, 91 | Moving off, positioning the car in the lane. |
| 107 | Applying the brakes. |
| 221 - 223 | Emergency vehicles and police officers |

## 1.0   Cockpit Check

A cockpit check is a check you carry out each time you enter the car to ensure all the controls are adjusted correctly before you drive off. Having done this, you will be in a position to use them properly and take full control of your vehicle.

Before you start the engine, make sure:

- All the doors are properly closed.
- Your seat is properly adjusted to give you comfort.
- You have fastened your seat belt.
- The handbrake is on and the gear is in neutral or park.
- The head restraint is well adjusted to give you maximum neck protection.
- Your exterior and interior mirrors are correctly adjusted.

When doing all the exercises in the following sections, switch off the radio/DVD player so you can concentrate. By hearing the sound of the engine, you can easily balance the acceleration and clutch pedals.

## 1.2 Starting the Engine

Before operating the starter, take a few minutes to study the ignition switch. It has four positions as shown in figure 3.1.

1. **LOCK** - The ignition switch has the anti-theft locking mechanism on the steering column that locks the steering wheel when you remove the key. For an automatic transmission gearbox, the key can only be removed when the gear lever is in park. To unlock it, insert the key. If you have a problem, giving the steering a gentle jerk as you insert the key will do the job.

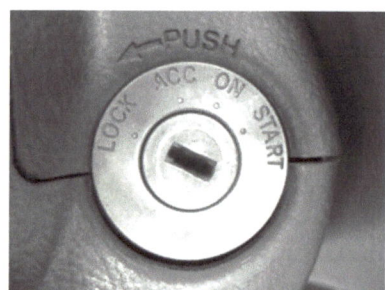

Figure 3.1 – Ignition switch.

2. **"ACC"** is short for accessories. Turning the key to this position sends the current to all the accessories such as fan and radio/DVD player.

3. **"ON"** - In this position, a host of warning lights in the instrument panel light up. This includes battery charging and oil pressure warning lights. You are able to operate electric windows and auto door locks. The lights turn off after the engine is running. However, if any warning light does not come on or turn off, have the problem investigated.

4. **START –** When you turn the key to start, power reaches the starter motor, which in turn causes the engine to start running. It has a spring so that immediately you let go the key, it returns to 'ON' position. Usually, the engine will easily start when all accessories such as radio and heater are switched off.

## Practice 1 – Starting the Engine

For a manual transmission system, start the engine only when the gear is in neutral, else the car will jerk away. For an automatic transmission gearbox, start the engine when the gear is in park.

Make sure you carry out the cockpit check. Insert the key into the ignition switch and turn it to **"ACC"**. Next, turn it further to '**ON**' position. As you do so, look at the instrument panel and see which warning lights are illuminated. Gently turn it further and when you hear the engine start, immediately let go the key. To switch off the engine, turn the key to '**LOCK**'.

If the engine fails to start, it may be because the spark plugs are dry. Press the accelerator gently to release a bit of fuel to the plugs. Then try again. Sometimes the engine may crank but fail to run. Try again by gently pressing the accelerator as you start the engine.

> ⚠ Holding on to the key in the START position after the engine has started running can damage the starter motor. Release it immediately you hear the engine running.

### 1.3   Finding the Holding Point

Carry out the next two exercises on a vehicle with a manual transmission gearbox. If you are using a vehicle with an automatic transmission gearbox, jump to Moving off Slowly and Stopping section.

Finding the holding or biting point is an important part of controlling the vehicle. Before a vehicle moves off, you raise the clutch while increasing pressure on the accelerator. As you raise the clutch pedal, you will find a biting point at a certain point. This is where the clutch attaches itself to the flywheel. Letting the clutch up further completes the connection of the clutch plate with the flywheel to rotate in unison and causes the vehicle to move forward.

## Practice 2 – Finding the Holding Point

To find the holding point, start the engine as usual. Push the clutch down and select 1st gear. Then gently press the accelerator. While your left heel is touching the floor, slowly raise the clutch. You will feel a force pushing your foot upward. Continue raising the clutch until you hear a slight drop in engine sound. This is the holding or biting point. Keep your foot still on the clutch for a moment. Next push the clutch down and select neutral. Switch off the engine.

Move on to the next exercises only after you have known how to find the biting point. The next sections will show you how to move off and stop smoothly.

> Another way you can tell that you have reached the biting point is when the bonnet is raised slightly.

Throughout your driving experience, you will continue to make use of this routine. Once you get used, you will not need to rely on the engine sound. It is not possible to hear the engine sound especially in heavy and noisy traffic.

The holding point is useful when you are going up the bridge and stopping frequently in heavy traffic. By making use of the clutch and accelerator, you will control the vehicle without applying the footbrake. Additional exercises on the holding point are in the next chapter.

## 1.4   Moving off slowly and Stopping

Your instructor will drive you to a road that is wide and less busy, with plenty of room for manoeuvering. Streets in residential areas are suitable. Alternatively, look for an open ground.

To gain control of moving in a straight line, use only the 2nd gear and maintain a speed limit not exceeding 20 km/ hr.  Repeat the exercise a number of times until you are able to move and stop smoothly.

### Practice 1 – For a Manual Transmission System

This exercise must only be done once you are able to operate the gears without looking down at them.

Start the engine to prepare the car for moving. Then gently press the accelerator and let go. Press the clutch and select gear one. While the vehicle is stationary, find the holding point and keep your foot still. Next, look around the vehicle and through the mirrors. Look over the right shoulder to make sure there are no vehicles in the blind spot. If there is traffic or pedestrians on the road, signal to alert them that you are joining the road. If the road is safe, release the handbrake.  Slowly take your foot off the clutch until the car begins to go forward. Gently press the accelerator to increase speed.

To steer in a straight line, hold the steering wheel at 0900 and 1500 hours. Keep to the normal driving position and look ahead. See figure 3.2 on page 17.

### Practice 2 – For an Automatic Transmission System

Turn the key to start the engine and press the footbrake. Next, press and hold the button on the gear selector and shift the lever to D. While your foot is still on the brake, look for approaching traffic. If necessary, double-check by looking over your shoulder. If traffic is on the road, signal to alert them of your intention to join the road. If it is safe, release the foot brake. The vehicle will start moving slowly. Gently press the accelerator to increase speed. Steer the vehicle close to the kerb.

## 1.5 Steering in a Straight Line

Figure 3.2 shows the correct position to maintain once you are on the road. Keep a distance of about one metre or the length of an open door from the kerb.

Once you are moving in a straight line, change to 2nd gear and accelerate to 20km/h. As you drive along, avoid looking at the bonnet or at the road in front of the bonnet. Instead, look well in advance for obstructions on the road and glance to the left side of the road for traffic signs. Be on the lookout for pedestrians too.

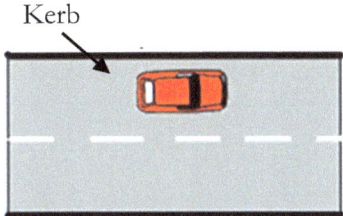

Kerb

Figure 3.2 – Keep a metre away from the kerb.

When passing parked vehicles (see figure 3.3), leave enough clearance between you and other vehicles. You will learn to judge this position through experience.

Like a soldier taking a sight before firing, you should develop the ability to judge this distance. When the vehicle is stationary, your instructor can stand near the left-fender at one foot, two feet and three feet at different times. While you are in the driver's seat, observe carefully how these distances appear to you.

Figure 3.3 - Leave enough space between you and parked vehicles.

## 1.6 Braking and Stopping

When approaching a junction, bend or obstruction, you should slow down early. If you wait until you are very close, you will be forced to apply a lot of pressure on the brake pedal. Doing so means you can stop within a safe distance when you are following other road users. When you stop in traffic queues, keep a distance of at least two metres.

**Practice 3 – For a Manual Gearbox**

Before you decide to stop, look through the rear-view mirror to check if there is traffic coming from behind. If necessary, give a left-hand signal. Then steer the vehicle to a safe place. Start applying gentle pressure on the footbrake. While the vehicle is still in motion, cover the clutch with your left foot – do not press it yet. As you approach where you intend to stop, press down the clutch. Further reduce the pressure on the footbrake so the vehicle comes to a smooth stop.

After stopping, select neutral gear. Apply the handbrake and switch off the engine.

> ⚠ When moving at a low speed, pressing the footbrake alone causes the vehicle to jerk away and the engine to switch off.

## Practice 4 – For an Automatic Gearbox

To stop the vehicle, look in the rear-view mirror to check if there is traffic coming from behind. If necessary, give a left-hand signal. Steer the vehicle to a safe place. Next, apply gentle pressure on the footbrake. Just before you stop, reduce the pressure on the footbrake to allow the vehicle to come to a smooth stop. When the vehicle has stopped, shift gear selector to P. Apply the handbrake and switch off the engine.

> 💡 Move off only when the road is safe. When you are likely to force other drivers to reduce speed or change direction, wait for a safe gap in traffic.

## 1.7 Stopping Smoothly

Very often, you will be slowing down or stopping frequently in traffic queues. To bring the vehicle to a smooth stop, you should start by judging correctly the distance remaining and apply gradual pressure on the brake pedal.

The following exercise shows you how to judge the distance and stop smoothly at a given point. After repeating this exercise a number of times, you should know exactly when to start applying the brakes.

Figure 3.5 – Mark your stopping point.

Find a field that is about 100 metres or more in length. Mount a plank into the ground at one end of the field. This will be your stopping point, see figure 3.5.

## Practice 5 – Stopping at a Given Point

Start the car at one end of the field and move at 25 km/h in 2rd gear. After covering half the distance, move your foot from the accelerator to let the vehicle slow down.

When there are 20 to 25 metres remaining, gently press the brake. Gradually increase the pressure as you draw nearer to the stopping line. Before you stop, press the clutch down and ease the pressure on the brake. The car should roll to the stopping point. When the bonnet is almost level with the plank, apply more pressure on the brake to bring the vehicle to a complete stop.

## 2.0  Steering Control

So far, you have concentrated on moving the car in a straight path. The next step is to learn how to steer the vehicle at bends and sharp corners without difficulties. You will use the pull-push method to make turns. As you turn, focus your eyes in the direction you are turning.

Find a wide field for this practice. Start the car as usual and drive away at below 20 km/h in 1st gear.

## 2.1  Turning Right

**Practice 1 – Turning Right**

Figure3.6 – Ready to steer right.

To turn right, slide your right hand to the top of the wheel (figure 3.6). Then pull the steering wheel down, at the same time, keeping your left-hand in the same position as the wheel slips through it. With your left hand, push the steering wheel up as you slide your right-hand to the top again. To position the car in a straight path, slide your left hand to the top of the wheel and pull it down.

While positioning the vehicle correctly in the lane, do not let the wheel spin through your hands.

When turning right, avoid cutting in as shown in figure 3.7. Instead, position the vehicle just left of the middle of the road. Then, as you turn, enter the left lane.

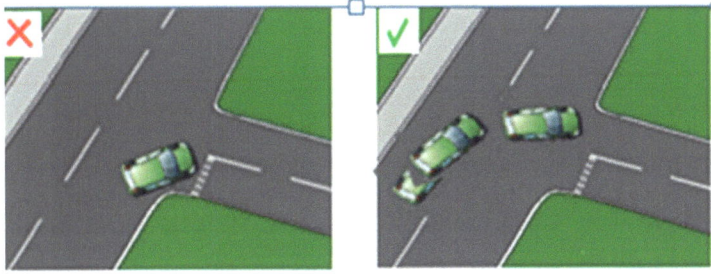

Figure 3.7 – Do not cut in when turning right.

## 2.2 Turning Left

**Practice 2 – Turning Left**

To turn left, slide your left hand to the top of the wheel (figure 3.8). As you pull the steering wheel down, keep your right hand in the same position as the wheel slips through it. Then push the steering wheel up with your right hand, as you slide your left hand to the top again. To position the car in a straight path, slide the right hand to the top of the wheel and pull it down.

Figure 3.8 – Ready to steer left.

⚠ Do not cross one hand over the other, or using one hand when turning to prevent an accident.

Figure 3.9 – Leave enough room for the rear wheel.

When negotiating at left corners, the rear wheels cut close in the bend. To avoid driving on the kerb, leave enough room as you turn, see figure 3.9. You will overcome this problem with more practice.

Holding the steering wheel with both hands during normal driving gives you full control of the vehicle, for example, at bends, when applying brakes, or when moving on slippery roads. On rough roads, hold it firmly so it does not steer out of control.

⚠ If you turn too early, the rear wheel can go over the kerb, or the side of the vehicle can hit into an object. Ensure to leave enough room.

On the other hand, holding the steering wheel with one hand while you are eating, drinking, or talking on the cell phone gives you limited control. It might look impressive, but it is almost impossible to react quickly to any hazard situation on the road.

## 3.0 The Mirror - Signal - Manoeuvre - MSM

The mirror - signal - manoeuvre, commonly known as MSM routine, is a sequence of three steps. We have already seen that mirrors enable you to see the positions of approaching traffic. Using this information, you decide whether it is safe to change lanes, overtake, move off, or stop.

## 3.1 Indicator Light Signals

The first step before you make any manoeuvre is to look through the mirrors and determine the positions of other road users. Then give a signal to alert them of your intentions. Remember that you do not give a signal to force your way. Rather, wait for other road users to respond before you manoeuvre.

If someone has not seen your indicator light, he or she will not give you room in which to manoeuvre. Table 6.1 below summarises the steps in a logical order.

| | | Table 6.1 |
|---|---|---|
| **Step** | | **Explanation** |
| 1 | Mirror | Start by looking ahead, or through the mirrors to check approaching vehicles or cyclists. |
| 2 | Signal | Next, turn on the indicator lights or give arm signal to alert other road users of your intentions. |
| 3 | Manoeuvre | When it is safe, change position, move off, or slow down. |

MSM routine ensures that you know what is happening ahead of you, to the sides and behind you. Make frequent use of mirrors in order to judge the positions and speed of other traffic coming from behind. This is important because you do not know who is likely to move where or who is alerting you to respond. Get in the habit of using mirrors before you do anything at all. However, be careful not to take your eyes off the road ahead for too long. Make quick glances then continue looking ahead.

It is advisable to start the mirror and signal sequence well in advance. By the time you reach the point at which you intend to manoeuvre, other road users behind and ahead of you would have known that you wish to change direction. Always double-check to confirm that they have seen you and responded correctly before you finally manoeuvre. Do not assume they know your intentions or have seen you.

In addition, if other road users are going to see you, avoid driving in their blind spots.

## 3.2  Arm Signals

Apart from using indicator lights, all competent drivers should use and correctly respond to arm signals given by other road users. They are effective during the light hours of the day.

Below is a table showing arm signals for slowing down, turning left and right.

| Table 6.3 | | |
| --- | --- | --- |
| **To slow down:** | **To turn left:** | **To turn right:** |
| Wave arm up and down. | Circle arm anticlockwise. | Point arm to the right. |

## 3.3  Using MSM at a Junction

When driving on a carriageway with multiple junctions, start signalling only after you have passed the second last junction (figure 3.10). Then slow down and keep as close as possible to the kerb.

If turning right, position your car just left of the middle of the road (figure 3.11). Be on the lookout for pedestrians crossing the road into which you are turning. If they are already crossing the road, give them the right of way.

Finally, after making the turn, return to the normal driving position,

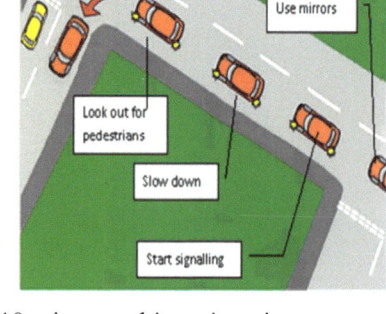

Figure 3.10 - Approaching a junction to turn left.

that is, about a metre from the left edge.

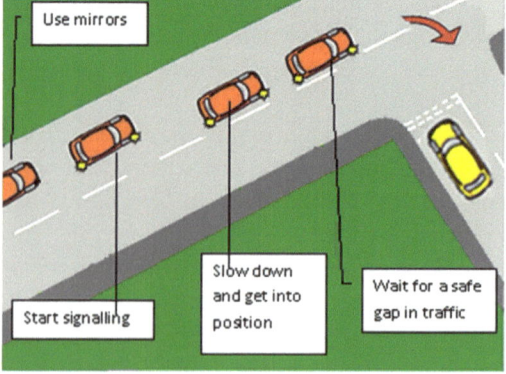

Figure 3.11 – Approaching a junction to turn right.

# 4 MOVING OFF AND CHANGING GEARS

The exercises in this chapter assume you have mastered finding the holding point you learnt in the previous chapter. This chapter explains in a step-by-step fashion how to coordinate the foot controls when moving up and down a hill. The chapter concludes with skills on defensive driving.

Study the following rules in the Highway Code before you proceed with this chapter.

| Rule No. | Rule |
|---|---|
| 99 - 100 | Narrow roads. |
| 108 - 111 | Emergency stops and brakes |
| 194, 259 - 263 | Weather and headlights. |

## 1.0  Moving off – Using Manual Gearbox
## 1.1  Moving Off Slowly and Changing Gears

By now, you should be familiar with the procedure for moving off, stopping and turning. In this section, you will continue with selecting appropriate gears when the car is in motion.

If you are having lessons on a vehicle with an automatic transmission system, jump to 'Controlling the Speed on Uphill Slopes' section on page 27.

### Practice 1 – Changing from 1st Gear to 2nd Gear

Find a fairly straight and wide road where there is less or no traffic. Move off in 1st gear and change into 2nd gear as soon as you can. Increase the speed to 20 km/h. Hold the wheel with both hands again. Keep your eyes on the road and drive on the left side of the road. Before reaching the end of the road, bring the car to a stop. Engage 1st gear and then neutral. While the engine is still running, change up the gears and move off again.

## Practice 2 - Changing from 2nd to 3rd and 4th Gears

Once you are comfortable with the first and second gears, continue with this exercise. Start the car in the usual way and move off. As soon as you exceed 20 km/h, change to 3rd gear. Then increase the speed to 30 km/h and change to 4th gear. Limit your road speed to between 30 and 40 km/h.

After the practice, stop the vehicle and go over any mistakes. Repeat the practice as required.

> When you hear the engine sound louder, you have exceeded the number of revolutions for that gear. Immediately change to the next high gear.

## Practice 3 – Braking and Changing Down through the Gears

To change down the gears, start by building up your speed to about 35 km/h in 4th gear. Then check the mirrors to ensure the road is safe. Start by braking gently to slow down to about 20 km/h. Release the brake and change into 3rd gear. Reapply the brake and slow down further. Change down to 2nd gear and check the mirrors once more. If the road is safe, build up the speed again, changing up the gears, until you reach 35 km/h.

Keep practising until you are confident.

## 1.2 Block Gear Changes

Changing down the gears in sequence as you have done is not necessary on modern vehicles. You can change down the gears in blocks, such as from 5th to 3rd, 4th to 2nd, or 3rd to 1st. Bear in mind that the gear you wish to engage should match the speed at which you are moving.

The benefits of this style of driving include better fuel economy, less overall wear and tear, less driver fatigue on long journeys and more steering control in emergencies.

> Changing down to a low gear while you are in high speed may cause the engine to rev unnecessarily high. Be careful!

## Practice 1 – Changing from 4th to 2nd Gear

Build up the speed to about 35 km/h in 4th gear. When the road behind is safe, apply the brake gently to slow down to about 20 km/h. Release the brake and change from 4th to 2nd. When the road is safe, build the speed up through the gears until you reach about 35 km/h. Practise again until you can do it smoothly and confidently.

## Practice 2 – Changing from 3rd to 1st Gear

You should be driving along at about 30 km/h in 3rd gear. When the road behind is safe, gently apply the brake to slow down until you have almost stopped. Press the clutch and keep it down. Release the brake so that the car keeps rolling forward very slowly. Just before the car stops, change from 3rd to 1st.

When the road is safe, move off again and accelerate, changing up through the gears until you reach about 30 km/h in 3rd gear. Practise again until you are confident enough.

## 2.0   Controlling the Speed on Uphill and Downhill Slopes

Ocassionally, you will find yourself going up a hill and probably starting the car while you are parked on an upward slope. When moving slowly in heavy traffic at a bridge for example, often you will be pulling up behind other vehicles. The procedure of coordinating the accelerator, clutch and handbrake comes in handy so you move off without rolling backwards.

If you are driving a vehicle with an automatic transmission gearbox, you do not have to worry about coordinating the three controls. As you move uphill or downhill, all you need to do is make use of the accelerator and brake pedals to slow down and increase the speed.

## 2.1   Uphill Starts

Find a wide and quiet road on a hill (figure 4.1). Drive slowly to an uphill slope and stop the car. While still applying the brakes, change to neutral or P and switch off the engine. Apply the handbrake and release the footbrake. Ensure that you keep about two metres away from the edge.

## Practice 1 – Method One

### Step 1 – Find the Holding Point

Start the engine and select 1st gear. Gently press the accelerator to give the engine power. Next, press the clutch and find the holding point. Check that there are no other road users nearby. If it is safe, release the handbrake. Keep your feet still and hold the car stationary for two or three seconds.

If the car moves forward, press the clutch down a little. If it rolls back, keep calm and raise the clutch slightly.

Continue to lower or raise the clutch until you find a point where the car comes to a stop.

Figure 4.1 – Practicing on an uphill slope.

### Step 2 – Moving off slowly with a Slipping Clutch

Follow the procedure in step 1 and then raise the clutch slightly until the car slowly moves forward. Now press the clutch down slightly and try to move forward very slowly without stopping.

### Step 3 – Regaining Control When You Roll Backwards

Repeat the procedure in step 1. Then push the clutch down slightly until the car starts to roll backwards. Let it roll two or three metres. To regain control, raise the clutch gradually until you can feel the car stopping.

> ⚠️ Letting the pedal up too far or too quickly may cause the engine to switch off or cause the car to jump forwards.

### Step 4 – Moving Off Quickly

Follow the procedure in steps 1 and 2 until the car is creeping forward. To accelerate and move off quickly, start by pressing the accelerator and then gently raise the clutch. Continue accelerating as you let the clutch up.

If the car jerks away, you need to press the accelerator a little harder or let the clutch up more slowly.

If the engine lets out a loud sound, let the clutch up a little more or use less pressure on the accelerator.

Remember to change into 2nd gear as soon as you have moved off.

### Practice 2 – Method Two

Suppose you are climbing a bridge and stopping occasionally. You may not make use of the handbrake. Drive in 2nd gear to the uphill slope. Apply the brakes to slow down and change down into 1st gear. While pressing the clutch, apply the brakes to stop. To move off, find the holding point. Then move your right foot from brake pedal to the accelerator. Now raise the clutch slightly until the car moves forward slowly. Once the car is in motion, let up the clutch completely and use more pressure on the accelerator to increase speed.

You will notice that as you transfer your foot from brake to accelerator the car may roll backwards slightly. It is okay if you have plenty of room behind.

## 2.2  Downhill Slopes

Driving slowly down the bridge is straightforward and much easier. To control the vehicle, use the clutch and brake pedals to stop behind other vehicles.

### Practice 1 – Controlling Speed Downhill

Drive slowly to a downhill slope and stop the car (figure 4.2). Start the engine again and select 1st, or 2nd gear if you are on a very steep slope. Apply the footbrake to hold the car and then let the handbrake off.

Check that there are no other road users nearby and then little by little let go off the footbrake to allow the car to roll slowly forwards. Keep the clutch down when moving at very low speeds but remember to raise it when you have released the footbrake completely.

Figure 4.2 – Control your speed when moving downhill.

A steep downhill slope may require you to stay in 2nd gear, otherwise 3rd gear is the highest to maintain the speed required. Travelling in neutral is not recommended because you eliminate engine braking. This will force you to use more pressure on the brakes, resulting in a short life span of brake pads.

## 3.0  Moving off – Using Automatic Gearbox

Find a fairly straight and wide road for your practice.

## Practice 1 – Moving Off Slowly

Start the engine and shift the gear to 'D'. Gently press the accelerator to give the engine power. To move off, release the handbrake and press the accelerator. Hold the steering with both hands as you move off slowly. Keep your eyes on the road and maintain the left side of the road. Maintain a 20 km/h speed. Before you reach the end of the road, bring the vehicle to a stop by applying the brakes. Engage 'P'. Without switching off the engine, engage 'D' and move off again.

## Practice 2 – Maintaining a Steady Speed

After going over practice 1 a number of times, you should be able to build enough confidence. With practice 2, increase the speed to 30 km/h.

Start the engine in the usual way and move off. Once you have held the steering with both hands, increase the speed to 30 km/h. To control the speed, apply gradual pressure on the brakes or press the accelerator. To stop the car, apply gradual pressure on the brakes until the car comes to a stop.

## 3.1 Moving on the Downhill and Uphill Slopes

Moving on the downhill and uphill slopes is as easy as ABC with an automatic vehicle.

## Practice 1 – Controlling the Speed Uphill

To stop on the uphill slope, simply apply the brakes to stop behind another vehicle. To move off, move your foot away from the brake and press the accelerator to gain speed. To move at very low speeds, do not press the accelerator unless you want to gain speed.

## Practice 2 – Controlling Speed Downhill

Drive slowly to a downhill slope and stop the car. Start the engine again and select 'D' gear. Check that there is no traffic coming from behind. When it is safe, release the handbrake, and allow the vehicle to roll slowly forward. You can apply the footbrake to control the speed.

## 4.0 When to Check the Instruments

Dials and warning lights in the instrument panel inform you of the status and performance of your vehicle. Most of the time, you will be alert by looking ahead. Whenever you can, take a quick look at one dial or check for any warning light.

Glancing at the speedometer enables you to monitor and control the speed of the vehicle as well as detect any problem as soon as it arises. Take warning lights seriously so you can avoid a breakdown or serious damage to the vehicle.

If the brakes have malfunctioned while you are driving, do not panic. Simply release the gas pedal and let the vehicle roll to a stop. As it slows down, change down to appropriate gears. In addition, an overheated engine or low oil pressure is equally a dangerous sign. You should immediately seek assistance.

Figure 4.3 – Check the instrument panel regularly.

## 5.0 Defensive Driving

Defensive driving is one of the vital skills you need to master. It deals with effectively managing an emergency on the road. This entails being alert to what is going on around you and responding correctly. When you are always alert, you will avoid braking hard or even avoid an accident. No doubt, our roads are full of surprises. Knowing what to do in a particular situation can save lives.

Examples are many. An oncoming vehicle can suddenly lose control and enter your lane. On the other hand, a child can suddenly run across the road and find himself right into your lane. In each of these circumstances, you should not panic but act quickly to avoid an accident. (See figure 4.4).

Defensive driving skills enable you to drive carefully and anticipate that things can go wrong anytime.

Always look well ahead, towards the sidewalk, and drive at a steady speed. In an emergency, you will not follow the mirrors-signal-manoeuvre because there is very little time to start looking around. You should have taken such precautions much earlier.

Figure 4.4 – Look out for children and other pedestrians.

## 5.1 Emergency Braking

The following exercises equip you with defensive driving skills.

## Practice 1 – Braking Firmly

Find a quiet and straight road. On the side of the road, place an object to mark the

29

point at which you will start applying the brakes.

You will be doing about 40 km/h. Before you reach the position you have marked, firmly hold the steering wheel with both hands. Immediately you reach it, quickly release the accelerator and slide your foot to the brake. Apply firm pressure but gradually. Keep your foot still, and as the car slows to a standstill, gradually release the pressure. At the same time, ensure that the car is moving in a straight line.

For a manual gearbox, press the clutch down to keep the engine running once the car has finally stopped. Once you have stopped, engage neutral or park, and apply the handbrake.

> ⚠ Press the clutch only when the vehicle has stopped. Pressing it earlier can make the vehicle difficult to control.

### Practice 2 – Emergency Stop

Repeat practice 1 above. When you reach the position you have marked, apply the brakes so you can stop the vehicle quickly. Be alert to recognise any signs of the wheels locking up. If the car starts to skid, ease the pedal slightly and reapply the brakes.

Figure 4.5 – Controlling a skidding car.

If the rear of the vehicle skids to the right as shown in figure 4.5, quickly and gently steer to the right to recover. On the other hand, steer to the left if the rear wheels skid to the left.

> ⚠️ Do not apply a lot of pressure suddenly as this may cause the wheels to lock and skid.

> ⚠️ BRAKE ONLY. When you apply the brakes, you cause the weight of the car to shift to the front. You should not turn the wheels and apply the brakes at the same time. Otherwise, the weight of the car can shift to one side and overturn.

## 5.2 Evasive Driving

Evasive driving is intended to help you gain a sense of control over your vehicle without using brakes. The following practice teaches you how to avoid one or more obstructions by taking a zigzag course.

### Practice 1 – Double Lane Change

Execute this exercise on an open field. In a straight line, place 5 to 6 cones or other suitable objects as shown in figure 4.6. Leave about 10 metres between each cone.

Figure 4.6 – Drive between the cones.

As you manoeuvre between the cones, do not move your hands from the steering wheel. Start by doing 15 km/h and approach the course from the right side, with both hands at 0800 hours and 0400 hours respectively. Maintain the same speed as you drive through the course, passing as close to the cones as possible.

At the first turn, steer the wheels into the bend as shown in figure 4.6. Immediately, be ready to enter the right bend. Again, steer the wheel into the opposite bend. Drive through and at the end of the course turn round and repeat the exercise from the opposite direction.

To steer correctly, focus your eyes in the direction you are moving and avoid driving too close to the cones.

Repeat the exercise, gradually increasing the speed to about 25 Km/h until you can drive through the course successively.

> To avoid hitting the cones, you should not turn early. Again over-steering will keep the vehicle swinging further and further out.

## 6.0 Controlling a Vehicle When a Tyre Burst Occurs

A front tyre burst is particularly dangerous when you are moving at a high speed as the driver can easily lose control of the vehicle. The noise from the tyre burst can cause panic to the unsuspecting driver. Sometimes he or she may not hear the sound if there is loud music inside the vehicle.

After a front tyre burst, the vehicle is pulled much harder to the side of the burst tyre. To handle the emergency, firmly hold the steering wheel with both hands and immediately release the accelerator. Then steer firmly in a straight path until the vehicle starts to lose speed and eventually comes to a stop. Do not try to apply the brakes because the vehicle can spin out of control.

In the case of a rear tyre blowing out, the vehicle may spin and overturn. To prevent this, firmly hold the steering wheel and steer in a straight path until the vehicle comes to a stop. Do not use the footbrake unless it is necessary, for example, when you have to avoid hitting into something. Applying the brakes will force the rear of the vehicle to spin, and you should be ready to correct the spin.

In most situations, tyre bursts are caused by poor quality tyres, incorrect tyre pressure, potholes, worn out tyres, or overloading. Some re-tread tyres are illegally manufactured in the back streets. Buying such tyres is seriously risking your own life and the lives of others. Even when driving at normal speed, defective tyres are unreliable and cannot withstand the weight of the vehicle. The solution to the problem is to ensure that your tyres are in perfect condition all the time.

## 7.0 Making a U-Turn

A U-turn is an 180° manoeuvre so that you start going in the direction you have just come from. On certain parts of a carriageway, U-turns are not permitted.

As you make a U-turn, ensure there is enough room to avoid going over the kerb or hitting any parked vehicles. Start by checking in the mirrors for approaching traffic, followed by giving a signal for the direction you are turning. Slow down and give way to oncoming traffic. When the road is safe, gently step on the gas to turn around slowly. Watch out for pedestrians and cyclists who may be crossing the road.

---

**Practice 1 – Making a U-Turn**

---

Set some objects on the ground at least a metre apart to create a semi-circle as shown in figure 4.7.

Approach the semi-circle from the left while driving at about 15 km/h in 1st or 'D' gear. Follow the steps for turning right and keep both hands on the steering wheel. If the turn is sharp, you will have to turn quickly. Ensure that the right rear wheel is not going over the objects.

After making a right U-turn successively, repeat the exercise, this time approaching the semi-circle from the right.

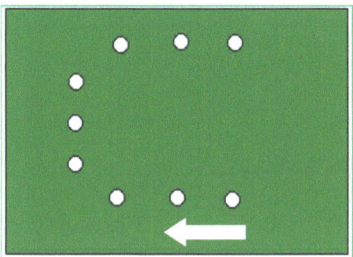

Figure 4.7 – Arc for making
a U-turn.

# 5 PARKING AND REVERSING

**P**arking safely and only in designated places cannot overemphasised. Improperly parked vehicles not only pose a danger to other road users, they also take up a lot of space. In addition, reversing is a tricky manoeuvre since your view is restricted and also often causes obstruction to other road users. Thus, you should take extra care by using the interior and exterior mirrors.

Study the following rules in the Highway Code before you proceed with the chapter:

| Rule No. | Rule |
|----------|------|
| 180 - 186 | Reversing |
| 198 - 199 | Waiting and parking |
| 201-202 | Parking and unloading |

## 1.0  Parking

Traffic rules permit drivers to park or stop in designated areas only. Very often, where parking or stopping is not permitted, signs will be displayed. Buses, taxis, motorcyclists, delivery goods vehicles have reserved parking areas. Other vehicles should not park or stop to pick up a passenger in these reserved areas.

Figure 5.1 - Park, facing uphill.

Take precautions when parking on an uphill or downhill slope by locking the front wheel against the kerb to prevent the vehicle from accidentally rolling away. When the vehicle is facing uphill, park close to the kerb on the left side of the road and turn the wheels to the right as shown in figure 5.1. Select a forward gear and apply the handbrake. On the other hand, when the vehicle is facing downhill, turn the wheels towards the kerb as shown in figure 5.2. Select reverse the gear and apply the handbrake.

Figure 5.2 - Park, facing downhill.

## 1.0 Reversing

Before learn how to park, the first thing you will learn is to reverse. Parking space on the streets in big cities is usually scarce. If you are fortunate to find a parallel parking, the vacant space may be too small to drive in. The only option left is to reverse in the space.

Many parking areas, especially at shopping centres, require you to reverse into a driveway before you move off. When you are reversing, take necessary precautions to avoid bumping into vehicles passing by. Always take time to look behind and around you before you reverse, and keep the speed down.

You can unbuckle your seatbelt so you can easily turn in your seat and look through the rear window. If you are not sure of what is behind, you may get out of the car to have a better look.

**Practice 1 – Reversing Slowly in a Straight Line**

Find a safe and quiet road where visibility is good and there are no obstructions on the pavement. Stop the car near the left kerb and let the engine to continue running. Cancel the indicator lights and make sure the wheels are aligned straight ahead. See figure 5.3. Your instructor can turn in his or her seat and look behind to make sure you are doing it correctly. Alternatively, he or she can stand on the pavement.

Before you start reversing, you should see the kerb and the white dotted lines through

Figure 5.3 – Reverse in a straight line.

the left and right mirrors. Engage reverse gear and place your hands at 10.00 and 14.00 hours. If the road is safe, reverse slowly as you look through the mirrors. When you have covered a distance of 20 metres, bring the car to a stop. Drive forward and repeat the exercise.

If you are not reversing in a straight line, stop the car. Drive forward to set the wheels in a straight line and start again. At the end of the exercise, you should reverse neatly without swinging from side to side.

For the practices that follow, first start in places where there are no parked vehicles. Once you have known how to carry out each exercise, repeat the same in an area where there are parked vehicles.

## Practice 2 – Reversing into a Road on the Left

Drive to a "T" junction and signal to warn other road users that you are about to stop on the left. Stop about ten to fifteen metres away from the corner and about half a metre from the kerb. Cancel your indicator lights.

Figure 5.4 – Check behind before reversing.

Look out for pedestrians or cyclists through the rear window. If they are present, give them way, see figure 5.4. If the road is clear, engage reverse gear. While looking through the left hand mirror, move off very slowly. When the corner is in line with the rear of your car, turn the wheel to the left. Since the front of the car will swing out towards the centre of the road, check for traffic approaching from both directions. If there is any coming your way, wait for it to pass. If it is safe, continue reversing very slowly. Ensure that the car is running parallel with the kerb. If a vehicle is coming from behind, stop the car. Continue reversing into the side road until you have done 20 metres. Finally, stop the car, engage neutral for manual gearbox or P for an automatic gearbox, and apply the handbrake.

Repeat the exercise until you can do it with confidence.

## Practice 3 – Parallel Parking – Reversing into a Parking Space

Reversing into a parking space requires you to pull up alongside the target car and park behind it. If you are doing this for the first time, look for three or more vacant spaces between two vehicles. Your instructor will guide into the parking space while you learn to calculate the clearance you need between the target car and yours.

As you approach the area, start by giving a left-hand signal to indicate your intention. Drive slowly until you bypass the vacant space and then stop as shown in figure 5.5. Leave a space of about one metre between your car and the target car. Cancel your signal. While stepping on the footbrake, engage reverse gear and look through the interior rear-view and external right mirrors for approaching traffic. If it is safe, begin to reverse slowly. When the

Figure 5.5 – stop next to target car.

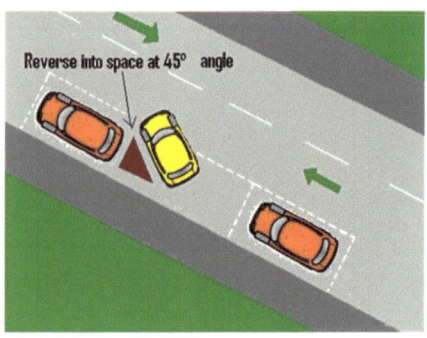

Figure 5.6 – Reverse into space at 45⁰.

rear bumper is in line with that of the target car, steer the car into the space. At this point, check the road ahead and behind. If it is safe, continue turning until you are moving into the space at an angle of 45 degrees (see figure 5.6). When your front bumper is level with the rear bumper of the target car, begin turning the wheel to the right. Ensure there is enough clearance between you and the target car. The car should now become parallel to the kerb. Then move forward to centre your car in the white box, leaving sufficient room for cars in front and behind to drive away easily.

After the entire manoeuvre, your vehicle should be parked as shown in figure 5.7.

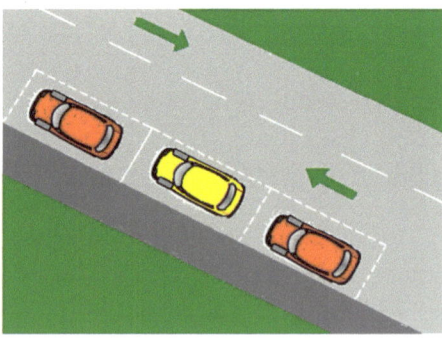

Figure 5.7– Centre your car into parking space.

## Practice 4 – Leaving Parallel Parking

Start the engine and check behind to ensure you have enough space for reversing. If it is safe, reverse until you are at least two metres away from the vehicle in front. Engage 1st gear or 'D' and give a right-hand signal. Look in front and behind for approaching traffic. If it is safe, turn the wheel as you move off, leaving enough clearance in front. Before you join the road, do a final check for traffic coming from behind. If it is safe, press the accelerator to move off and steer the car to a normal driving position.

## Practice 5– Reversing From "Angle" Parking

Start the engine, and then look behind for pedestrians, cyclists and other vehicles. If the road is safe, start to reverse in a straight line until the front bumper is clear of the rear bumper of the vehicle on the right. Then steer the wheel to the left. When you are well clear from the parking lot, stop the car. See figure 5.8. Select 1st or 'D' gear and move off. You should not enter the right lane while reversing (Figure 5.9).

Figure 5.8 – Reversing from 'angle' parking.

Figure 5.9 – Do not reverse into the right lane.

## Practice 6 – Reversing into a Parking Bay

This manoeuvre is popular among examiners to test your reversing skills. It is usually the first test you carry out before you go on the road. Make sure you can do the following two exercises accurately.

Find an empty parking bay, and place some objects (such as cones) to act as guide as shown in figure 5.10 by the dotted lines.

**Method 1**

Approach the parking bay and park directly opposite. Then engage reverse gear and look through the exterior rear view mirrors and start reversing slowly, straight into the bay. Continue checking the position of the car, and if the car is out of line, turn the wheels to correct this. When the front of the car is inside the bay, stop the car.

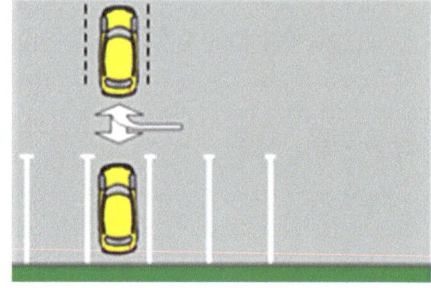

After a few seconds, engage 1st gear or D gear. Move off and turn right, ensuring you do not cut in. Stop the car after covering a distance of 3 to 4 metres. Engage neutral for a manual gearbox or P for an automatic gearbox, apply handbrake and switch off the engine.

5.10 – Reverse slowly into a parking bay.

---

**Practice 7 - Reversing into a Parking Bay**

**Method 2**

Drive slightly past the target bay. Leave a space of at least one metre between your car and the bay. See figure 5.11. Engage reverse gear and look around the vehicle. When the way behind is safe, look through the exterior mirrors and start reversing slowly, steering into the bay. As you enter the bay (figure 5.12), look through the mirrors to ensure you have

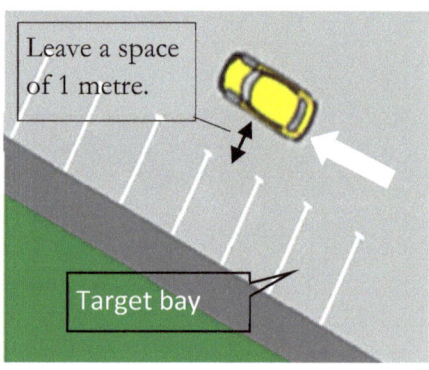

Figure 5.11 – Drive past target bay.

enough clearance on both sides. Continue reversing and keep looking. Make sure the rear wheels do not touch the white lines.

Once you are inside the bay, straighten the wheels. Stop the car when the front of the car is inside the bay, see figure 5.13. After a few seconds, engage 1st or D gear. Move off and turn left, following the same path. After covering the same distance as in practice 6 above, stop the car.

Figure 5.12 – Reverse slowly into the bay.

Engage neutral for manual gearbox or P for an automatic gearbox, apply the handbrake and switch off the engine.

At first, it is okay to move forwards and backwards at the entrance to the bay. However, you should enter the bay without difficulties after a few practices.

Before you are done, repeat the exercise 6, this time entering the parking bay first and reversing into an area you have set up with your own objects.

Figure 5.13 – Stop and park.

## 2.0 Parallel Parking

In parallel parking, you simply drive forward or reverse into a parking space.

### Practice 1 – Parallel Parking

Find a parking area that has about three vacant spaces. See figure 5.14. To park in parallel, drive slowly as you approach the parking area. Give a left hand signal and reduce the speed further. Leave enough clearance if there is a vehicle parked at a point you will be turning into the parking area. Steer left and once you are close enough to the kerb, turn the wheels to the right to make the car run parallel with the kerb. Gently apply the brakes to bring the car to a stop. Centre the car in the box to give enough room to vehicles in front and at the rear to move off safely. Engage neutral, apply the handbrake, and switch off the engine.

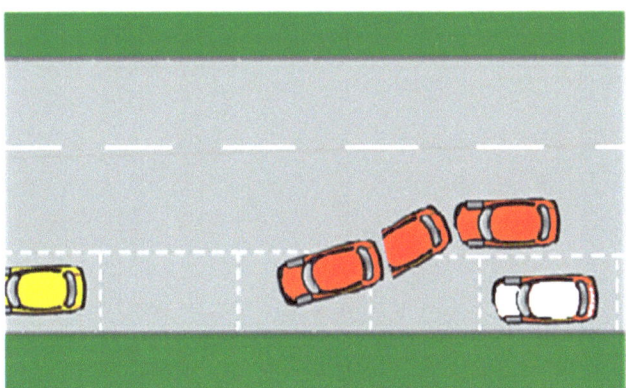

Figure 5.14 Driving into a parking space.

Repeat the exercise until you can do it comfortably.

## 3.0 "Angle" Parking

"Angle" parking is also an easy manoeuvre since vehicles enter parking space in a diagonal fashion.

### Practice 1 – "Angle" Parking

As you approach the parking area, use mirrors to check for other traffic. Give a left hand signal to warning them you intend to park. Reduce speed as you look well ahead for a vacant space. Next, steer into the space, ensuring you leave enough clearance on the right side, see figure 5.15. At the same time, use the left-hand exterior mirror to ensure you do not cut in. When the front of the car is at least 30cm from the kerb, stop the car.

When you have parked safely between the white lines, any door you open should not bump into a vehicle on either side.

Figure 5.15 – Park into space correctly.

### Practice 1 – Reversing in a Road

Certain roads have no open spaces where you can turn left or right to go back. The only option left to you is to turn around in a road. Your instructor can stand near the pavement to monitor your manoeuvres. Choose a quiet road with good visibility.

Figure 5.16 – Stop on the left.

Figure 5.17 – Directly face the kerb.

To reverse in the road, stop on the left where the pavement is clear of streetlight or telephone poles. See figure 5.16. Cancel indicator lights and look around to ensure the road is clear. Look over your right shoulder to check the blind spot.

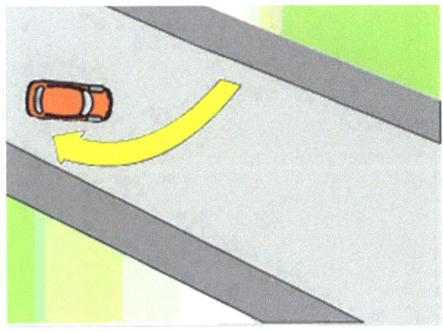

Figure 5.18– Reverse across the road.

If the road is clear, go forward in 1st or D gear and steer to the right. The car should face the kerb at right angles as shown in figure 5.17. When the front bumper is about one metre from the kerb and you are still moving very slowly, turn the steering wheel briskly to the left.

Once the front wheels are close enough to the kerb, press the clutch down and apply the brakes. Select a reverse gear and find the biting point. Check in all directions to make sure the way is clear. If clear, move off slowly across the road, turning the steering wheel as far to the left as it will go. See figure 5.18. When you have enough room in front, turn the wheel briskly to the right. Stop the car before you hit the kerb. Select 1st or D gear and drive forward, turning the wheel to the right. You should now steer to the left side of the road.

> Reversing into a road is appropriate in less busy areas. You should not reverse in areas where you are likely to obstruct traffic.

# 6 MANOEUVRING AT JUNCTIONS

This chapter looks at road skills, vis-à-vis how to approach busy and complex junctions, how to join, leave and cross these junctions.

Study the following rules in the Highway Code before you proceed with this chapter:

| Rule No. | Rule |
|----------|------|
| 121, 166 - 172 | Junctions and busy roads |
| 173- 175 | Traffic lights and police officers |
| 176, 177 | Turning left and right. |
| 178, 179 | Roundabouts |
| 203 - 208 | Level crossing |

## 1.0   Approaching Junctions

To gain more driving experience, you need to practice on a wide variety of roads and junctions. These include roundabouts, T-junctions, crossroads, railway crossing, dual carriageways, etc.

Some junctions have an open view that allows you to see clearly quite early vehicles approaching from both the right and left directions. However, others have a restricted view because of parked vehicles, buildings, or trees. In every case, approach each junction with caution and make use of MSM routine early. Look out for signs that may require you to respond accordingly and reduce speed. Where possible, change to the correct lane in good time.

If parked vehicles block your view, edge out a little to have a clear view of approaching vehicles. The distance between you and oncoming vehicles may seem vast, but remember that traffic on major roads will be moving very fast. Before you decide to enter the main road, take time to judge their speed and wait until the road is safe.

At the same time, do a final check to confirm there are no cyclists or motorbikers hidden behind a vehicle that is turning left. See figure 6.1. In addition, watch out for somebody who might be overtaking at the junction.

Figure 6.1 – Look out for motorcyclists hidden behind a vehicle.

Sometimes, an approaching vehicle may have its indicator lights on. Do not be quick to assume it is turning left until you see the driver showing signs of doing so.

Figure 6.2 – Stay back and allow a long vehicle to complete the manoeuvre.

Join the road only when it is safe. As you do so, do not interrupt the flow of traffic.

In addition, long vehicles require a lot of space when turning. You will have to stay back if you see one emerging from a side road or turning into the side road, see figure 6.2.

 Be on the lookout for cyclists and bikers who are usually difficult to see.

## 1.1 Turning Right

Turning right is one of the sensitive manoeuvres on busy roads. You normally come to position your vehicle just left of the middle of the road, leaving enough room for other traffic going straight. On wider roads, you are likely to find lane markings that guide you into position. If there are no markings, you should still leave enough room for vehicles coming from behind to pass on the left side.

When you intend to turn right, check your mirrors and give a signal as early as possible. Begin to slow down into position and stop where you will be turning, see figure 6.3. Then wait for a safe gap in the oncoming traffic. Also, make sure there is no one trying to overtake you on the right side.

Position the vehicle correctly.

Figure 6.3 – Position the car to allow other traffic to pass on the left.

## 1.2 Turning Left

When you are about to turn left, do not overtake other vehicles to avoid braking hard a short time later. Use mirrors in good time and then start by giving a left-hand signal.

Where a filter lane is available, occupy it early enough, and look out for approaching traffic on the main road. Give way to cyclists and pedestrians who are already crossing the lane or side road.

If you are following a cyclist

Figure 6.4 – Slow down and give way to a cyclist.

as shown in figure 6.4, slow down and allow him or her to proceed safely. Do not sound your car horn, which can cause him to panic. If you are following a vehicle that is turning left, reduce your speed. Be patient and allow the vehicle in front to complete a turn. Do not be tempted to pull out to the right and pass, as it is not safe especially at busy junctions.

> It is unnecessary to swing out to the right before turning into the side road. Doing so is dangerous to oncoming traffic.

## 1.3  Crossroads

Traffic approaches a crossroads from two or four directions. As you draw closer to the junction, you will see road markings or upright signs indicating which road users have priority over others. However, it is always better to take precautions and look out for road users who may continue driving when they do not have the right of way. By slowing down, you will have time to observe in the side roads before you proceed.

In the absence of traffic lights, you will find four-way stop signs, in which case all traffic approaching the junction is required to stop. Here is where you exercise patience. A vehicle that arrives first is given priority to move off, followed by the second, et cetera. When two vehicles arrive at the same time, one should give way to another. Eye contact with other drivers is, therefore, important so that you give each other a chance to move off safely.

### Turning Right – Right Side to Right Side

Right side to right side manoeuvre occurs when two vehicles from opposite directions arrive at a crossroads simultaneously and both intend to turn right. See figure 6.5. Before you turn, bypass the other vehicle and position your car to drive behind it. Similarly, the other driver will pass you and position his or her vehicle to drive behind your car. If you are following a vehicle that is turning right, give way to the one turning right.

Figure 6.5 - Right side to right side manoeuvre.

## *Turning Right or Going Straight*

When you intend to turn right from a minor road, slow down and stop before the white dotted or solid lines. Wait for a safe gap in the main road, at the same time, give way to vehicles that are going straight (figure 6.6). Do not enter the main road while it is not clear because you will obstruct traffic that may be approaching the junction from other directions.

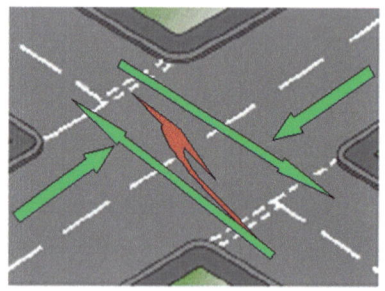

Figure 6.6 – Red arrow stands for a vehicle that gives way to other traffic before turning.

If you are going straight, proceed across the major road only when you have checked that the road you are joining ahead is clear.

⚠ If you find yourself in a wrong lane, do not change into another while at the junction.

## 1.4  Level Crossings

Trains may seem to move very slowly because of their sheer size. As a result, many drivers are tempted to cross the level crossing in spite of the train sounding a warning. Since the train has no emergency brakes, level crossings are the most dangerous junctions.

Some crossings have barriers, red flashing lights, or stop signs that prevent traffic from going forward when a train is approaching (see figure 6.7). Flashing lights are turned on to alert road users of the approaching train. Besides the first two control devices mentioned earlier, a

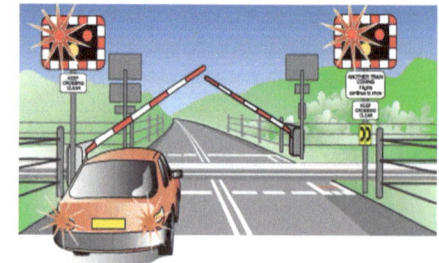

Figure 6.7 – One type of level crossing.

mandatory "STOP" sign directs you to stop whether a train is approaching or not. Always approach the railway crossing with care. You should, under no circumstances, overtake at this junction.

After stopping before the white lines, look in both directions of the rail line and listen for a sound of a train. Sometimes an attendant is available, and when he or she gives a warning sign, you should stop well away from the crossing.

## 2.0 Driving on Dual Carriageways

Figure 6.8 – A dual carriageway.

A dual carriageway divides a road into several lanes, separated by a central reservation as shown in figure 6.8. Each side of the road has two or more lanes on which traffic moves in the same direction. You should stay in the left lane and leave the right lane for overtaking. As soon as you have overtaken, return to the left lane.

On a three-lane carriageway, use the middle or right lane to overtake and return to the left lane to complete the manoeuvre. As you approach the exit point, change to the correct lane in good time.

Where there is a lot of traffic, use mirrors to judge the positions of other vehicles. Always look out for motorbikes that squeeze their way between other traffic. You should avoid driving in the blind spot of other drivers who cannot see you.

### *Turning Right on a Dual Carriageway*

When you are turning right into a dual carriageway, treat each carriageway as a separate road (figure 6.9). Before you cross any road, look in either direction for approaching traffic. You may wait in the middle if the reservation is big enough to accommodate your vehicle. Otherwise, wait in the side road until you can cross both carriages at the same time. If there is a vehicle ahead of you, be patient and allow it to

Figure 6.9 – Turning right on the dual carriageway.

complete a turn. Then you can move forward and stop before the white dotted lines.

Since traffic will be moving at high-speed, join in quickly and occupy the left lane without obstructing or slowing down the flow of traffic.

## 3. Roundabouts

Roundabouts are circular junctions with one or more lanes depending on the size. They are simple junctions but can be dangerous especially when you do not slow down and give way to traffic in the roundabout.

Treat roundabout just as any other junctions. Approach the roundabout cautiously and decide well in advance which exit you will be taking. Then check your mirrors, give signal and slowdown in the correct lane. If you find traffic in the roundabout, stop before the white dotted line. Look out for cyclists already in the roundabout and let them pass.

On your approach to a roundabout, white dotted lines merge into a single solid line. This means you should not change to another lane. If you need to do this, make sure you do so well in advance.

Blue car: going straight.

Green car: turning right.

Red car: turning left.

Figure 6.10 – How to exit a roundabout.

### Turning Left – First Exit

If you intend turning left, approach the roundabout in the left lane and signal left. If there is a vehicle in front of you, wait for it to leave. Then wait for oncoming traffic to pass before joining. When the road is clear, move off and steer left to leave the junction. See a red car in figure 6.10. At times, you may enter the roundabout without stopping as long as there is no traffic. Nevertheless, reduce speed and look out for traffic in the roundabout.

### Going Straight Ahead – Second Exit

Approach the roundabout in the left or right lane. Since you are going straight through the roundabout, you do not need to give a signal yet. See a blue car. As you move in the roundabout, make sure you stay in the same lane. After passing the first exit, give a left-hand signal and go straight ahead.

## *Turning Right – Third Exit*

When turning right, approach in the right lane and give a signal (green car). When it is safe, enter the roundabout and keep to the right. After passing the second exit, give a left-hand signal. On exit, you may stay in the same lane or change to the left lane. Before you change to another lane, look over your shoulder to make sure the lane you are joining is safe.

> ⚠ Do not occupy left lane if you intend to use a third exit, otherwise you will interfere with traffic going straight.

## 4.0 Junctions Controlled by Traffic Lights

While traffic light is still green and you are some distance away, approach the junction with care. Try to judge correctly if, by the time you reach the junction, the signal is likely to change to red. Do not increase the speed in order to 'beat' the traffic lights.

When amber light appears, prepare to slow down and stop. You may proceed only if you have already past the stop line. Always prepare to stop when traffic lights are about to change from AMBER to RED.

### *Using Filter a Lane*

Where a GREEN ARROW light signal is available for traffic turning right or left, you should move into the filter lane early enough (Figure 6.11). Provided the signal is GREEN, you may proceed in the direction indicated even if the main traffic light signal is RED. Otherwise, you should wait in the filter lane until the green arrow light turns on. Watch out for pedestrians crossing the lane and give them way. As you emerge from the lane, always watch out for cyclists or motorcyclists who are often difficult to see.

Figure 6.11 - Junction with filter lanes.

# 7 HOW TO AVOID ACCIDENTS – PART ONE

This chapter looks at lane discipline, separation distance, speeding and overtaking. Competency in these areas, being alert at all times, concentrating and responding correctly to other road users constitute part of good road skills.

Study the following rules in the Highway Code before you proceed with this chapter:

| Rule No. | Rule |
|---|---|
| 52 - 54 | Animals |
| 95 - 98, 113 - 114 | Speed limit and separation distance. |
| 119, 120, 123, 125, 126, 132 | Lane discipline |
| 90, 133 – 138,141 – 143 | Overtaking |
| 140 | Passing cyclists |
| 149 - 165 | Pedestrians and pedestrian crossing |

## 1.0   Lane Discipline

Before joining the main road, you should always wait for a safe gap. Then occupy the left lane where you can increase your speed and position the vehicle correctly to give other road users enough room to pass (figure 7.1). But driving on the white lines takes up more space than is necessary and makes it difficult for other road users in other lanes to manoeuvre properly.

When driving on a road with multiple lanes, reserve the right lane for overtaking. However, you may pass in the left lane if traffic in the right lane is moving slower than you are.

As you drive along, look well ahead to see what is going on with other traffic. That way, you will avoid changing lanes unnecessarily and applying the brakes suddenly.

If you need to overtake slow moving vehicles, begin by using mirrors and signal to indicate your intentions to other road users. Finally, look over your shoulder and give yourself plenty of space as you change to another lane. After overtaking, return to the left lane.

Figure 7.1 – Position the car correctly in the lane.

## 2.0 Meeting Other Traffic

On busy streets, remain alert and drive safely when you meet other road users. On residential and school streets, slow down and drive at recommended speed. Expect people to be about or crossing the road. Look out for children who may run out from behind parked cars or buses. Avoid frightening them by sounding the horn loudly.

In business centres, the road is likely to be narrower than usual because vehicles park on either side of the road (figure 7.2). Take necessary precautions as you pass by, cross, or even overtake other road users.

Figure 7.2– Drive slowly in busy areas.

If there is an obstruction, such as a parked car on your side of the road, slow down and give priority to oncoming traffic. Do not increase speed and try to beat the oncoming vehicle. In some cases, the oncoming driver may signal to you to proceed. It is, therefore, necessary to keep eye contact with other road users. Then pull out and drive in the centre of the road. Return to your lane after passing the obstruction.

## 3.0 Separation Distance

A separation distance is the amount of space you are required to maintain between you and the vehicle you are following. It acts as a safety net and, irrespective of how fast you are moving, when you apply the brakes you will stop within a safe distance.

If you notice that a driver behind you is getting too close, do not be under pressure to accelerate. Instead, allow them to overtake you if they intend to.

Table 7.1 below shows the speeds and recommended distances to maintain. For example, when you are driving at 50 km/h, your separation distance to maintain is a minimum of 25 metres. It is made up of the distance you take to respond and the distance the vehicle will travel after you have started applying the brakes. Some people respond faster than others. Therefore, the total distance for the speed in kilometres per hour is a minimum. The speed is in direct proportion to distance. The faster you are driving, the greater the distance to maintain. When driving at 100Km/h, you will keep a distance of 80 metres, or better still, the length of a football field. Failure to maintain a separation distance is one of the causes of road traffic accidents.

| Table 7.1 (Courtesy of Ministry of Communications and Transport) | | | |
| --- | --- | --- | --- |
| Typical Stopping Distances (Approximate speeds) | | | |
| Speed (Km/h) | Thinking distance(metres) | Braking distance(metres) | Total(in metres) |
| 30 | 6 | 6 | = 12 |
| 40 | 8 | 10 | = 18 |
| 50 | 10 | 15 | = 25 |
| 60 | 12 | 21 | = 33 |
| 70 | 14 | 29 | = 43 |
| 80 | 16 | 38 | = 54 |
| 90 | 18 | 48 | = 66 |
| 100 | 20 | 59 | = 79 |
| 110 | 22 | 71 | = 93 |

You can measure the separation distance using a simple method. Pick out an object, for example, a streetlight pole, or a road sign along the side of the road. It should take you a minimum of two seconds to reach it after the vehicle you are

Figure 7.3—How to measure a separation distance.

following has gone past it. See figure 7.3. You can say the following sentence in two seconds to help you determine the separation distance: "The number you have dialled". If you reach the sign before that time, then you are very close. Reduce your speed to extend the distance.

However, a number of factors come into play when considering the separation distance. These include the condition of the road (wet or dry), size of a vehicle, the condition of brakes, the condition of tyres and your quick response. On a wet day, the road surface becomes slippery. Refrain from driving at high speeds because when a layer of water comes between the tyres and road surface, you will be unable to brake and steer the wheel effectively. When the brakes are wet, the braking distance increases and may cause one side of the vehicle to brake more than the other. On a very hot day, the road surface becomes soft. In such instances, you have to increase the separation distance to four seconds. Furthermore, when visibility is bad, you will extend the distance further and turn on the headlights so that other road users can see you. If the weather is extremely bad, it is safe to park until the condition improves.

Maintaining a separation distance is also helpful when you meet obstructions, such as a broken down vehicle. You will be ready to slow down and let others pass, or signal to pull out. Therefore, avoid following another vehicle very close (figure 7.4).

Figure 7.4 - Do not get too close behind
a vehicle.

## 4.0 Over Speeding

Over speeding has always been a common problem on our roads. While some over speed out of excitement, others simply disregard the rules in the Highway Code.

Your road speed depends on a number of things: road condition, weather, and traffic flow, time of day and presence of  pedestrians. Some terrains are not suitable for speeding in excess of 100 kilometres per hour. Bends, for example, are hazardous spots where you can easily lose control of the vehicle. Because you cannot see around the bend, see figure 7.4, prepare for the unexpected. Hidden from sight could be a broken down vehicle or a fallen tree blocking the road.

I must slow down.

Figure 7.4 – Drive carefully at a bend.

When approaching heavy traffic, check the speed of other traffic and match your speed to fit safely into the traffic flow. But if driving at high speeds, you will be forced to apply sudden breaks, or zigzag your way in the traffic flow. This is not safe. It also disturbs and inconveniences other traffic.

Where a road has a number of humps intended to reduce the speed of traffic, maintain the reduced speed and do not overtake other traffic along this stretch of the road.

Cattle

Wild animals

On the highways or country roads, look out for warning signs indicating that you are in an area where animals normally cross the main road.

## 5.0 Overtaking

Overtaking is another cause of many traffic accidents. In most cases, accidents occur because someone made a wrong judgement or failed to control the vehicle after overtaking. One should not ignore the simple steps to follow before overtaking. Always double-check and take extra care, and if in doubt, wait a little longer.

Look out for road markings and signs that do not permit you

I must first pass by the junction before I start signalling.

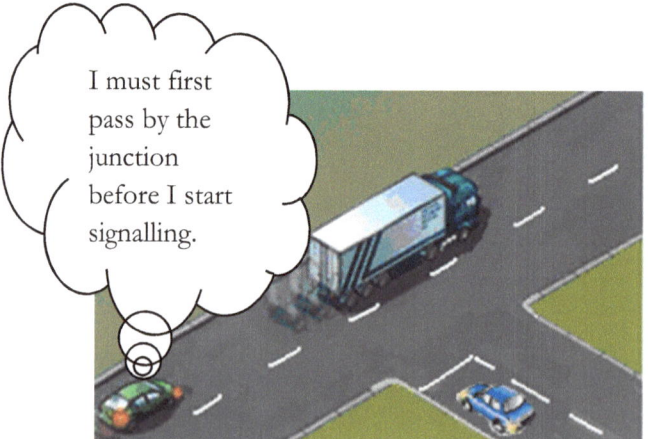

Figure 7.5 - Avoid overtaking at a junction.

to overtake. Avoid overtaking in areas such as junctions, near pedestrian crossings, at bends, the brow of a hill, or on white solid lines. Sometimes, drivers want to change lanes when they are approaching a pedestrian crossing.

However, a white solid line prohibits drivers to take this manoeuvre. You should not ignore warning signs that prohibit you to make an illegal move.

When you attempt to overtake near a junction, very likely a driver in the side road may think you wish to turn right. See figure 7.5. Because he pays attention to vehicles approaching from his right, he may not see you until after he has emerged from the side road.

Be careful when drivers moving at low speeds give you a signal to overtake them. Do not start the manoeuvre until you have double-checked the road is clear of oncoming traffic.

To overtake, begin by using mirrors to see what is happening behind. If no other vehicle intends to overtake, position the car so that you have a clear view ahead. If there is oncoming traffic, take enough time to judge the distance and their speed. Do not underestimate the speed of oncoming traffic. Also, ensure that you are on a stretch of the road that is straight and safe. Avoid pulling out suddenly to overtake.

When you have decided to overtake, start by giving a signal. To make sure other road users have seen you, give them enough time. Then move into position and quickly pass the vehicle, leaving sufficient room on your side. Then make a gradual return to your lane. Do not cut in on the vehicle you have just overtaken, otherwise, you may force the driver to apply the brakes. This usually happens when you do not have enough room in which to manoeuvre because of oncoming traffic. The green arrow in figure 7.6 shows the correct path to take when overtaking.

Figure 7.6 - Move into position and pass the vehicle quickly.

For this manoeuvre, always ask yourself this question. "Is it safe to overtake now?" If you decide to abort overtaking, do not wait until it is too late. Abort as soon as you realise the road is not safe. You should take extra care when driving at night on a road with no streetlights.

Some drivers may increase the speed when they see you overtaking. If this happens, do not engage in a car race. Reduce your speed and return to your lane.

## 6.0  Pedestrians and Cyclists

Pedestrians and cyclists, too, have a place on the roads just as any other road users. Unfortunately, they often face a great risk of being run over. Every good driver should be concerned about their safety when they are seen on the road. Expect to meet the young and elderly persons, including the blind and sick pedestrians who are all vulnerable. The best way to avoid a fatal accident or reduce the risk of injury is by reducing your speed rather than sounding the horn while driving at high speed.

Figure 7.7 - Give pedestrians already crossing the right of way.

At junctions, look out for pedestrians crossing the road into which you are turning. If they are already crossing it, give them the right of way, as shown in figure 7.7. Normally, they will not look behind but pay attention to vehicles coming from the left side. Do not intimidate them by sounding the horn, otherwise, they will panic and run across the road.

At pedestrian or pelican crossings, allow children and other people to cross the road safely, see figure 7.8. Do not intimidate them by screeching the brakes or by forcing them

Figure 7.8 – Stop at Zebra crossing to allow pedestrians to cross the road.

58

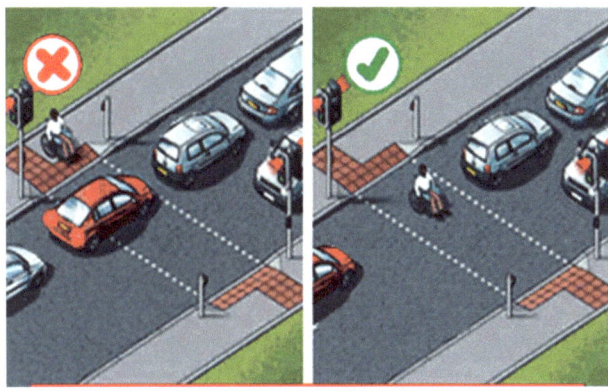

Figure 7.9 – Keep the crossing clear.

to hurry across the road. This is unfair and unnecessary trouble! Move off only when they are on the sidewalk. When moving in a traffic queue, keep the crossing clear (figure 7.9)

In the absence of pedestrian crossing, drive slowly and look out for pedestrians who may be crossing the road from behind stationary vehicles. The highways, too, may not have pedestrian crossings. Do not assume that people crossing the carriageway have seen you. Some are hard of hearing and possibly blind. Do not assume they have seen you, but take the first step to warn them that you are there. When they do not respond, take necessary measures to avoid any mishap.

On roads with multiple lanes, pedestrians usually occupy each lane at a time as they move across the road. Slow down as you drive in these densely populated areas.

The number of cyclists has increased on our roads in recent years. This means you should be careful as they tend to drift from side to side as they cycle along. When approaching them, drive near the centre of the road so that they have enough room in which to manoeuvre. See figure 7.10. It is also unlikely that they will hear a vehicle approaching from behind when cycling in the direction of the wind. Alert them by sounding the horn and be

Figure 7.10 - Drive near the centre as you overtake a cyclist.

ready to reduce your speed. If you do not warn them, they might decide to move across the road without first looking behind.

# 8 HOW TO AVOID ACCIDENTS – PART TWO

By the time you start reading this chapter you will be two steps away from taking your driving test. This chapter looks further at what it takes to become a responsible driver. As you have already seen, adhering to traffic rules and applying the knowledge and skills you have acquired so far helps to avoid accidents.

Study the following rules in the Highway Code before you proceed with the chapter:

| Rule No. | Rule |
|---|---|
| 101, 105, 122 | Patience and consideration |
| 139, 147, 148 | Avoiding accidents and using mobile phones |
| 188, 189, 191, 258 | Driving at night |
| 209 - 213 | Breakdown and use of reflective triangles |
| 214 - 220 | Dealing with accident situations |

## 1.0   Patience and Consideration

Patience is an important virtue that every driver should possess. It is the ability to wait upon others and withstand a usually uncomfortable situation without being worked up. This means restraining yourself from reacting out of proportion to a particular situation.

In the first place, the road itself is a nuisance. You will experience delays, or obstructions, for example. You will come across drivers you think have a bad attitude or deliberately disregard traffic rules. Furthermore, you will find out that elderly drivers react much slower than younger drivers. Do not be quick to condemn those you think are less skilful than yourself. Remember that every road user, whether young or old deserves respect. Understanding the characteristics of different drivers may help you to remain calm.

Reacting with patience to mistakes made by others reveals a spirit of maturity. But an impatient driver is not willing to wait and he fails to observe traffic lights. He is unkind and aggressive to others for committing mistakes even too small to be worth of consideration. He may also think that pedestrians are a nuisance when he is moving at high speeds. In anger, he blows his horn or screams at others because he finds others too slow.

In case someone decides to turn right without giving you sufficient warning, hold back and let him complete the turn. Avoid getting irritated, but respond calmly. If you can, try to manoeuvre in such a way you will avoid any mishap.

Furthermore, watch out for drivers emerging from a side road. You may have the

Figure 11.1- Do not block access to a side road.

right of way, but when a driver suddenly enters the main road, slow down and hold back. As you drive along, be considerate and courteous to other road users. Give way to those who want to change lanes or turn into a side road.

## 2.0 Mobile Phones and Music

In recent times, the use of mobile phones by drivers behind the wheel has reached epidemic levels. Some have become very addicted to phones they deliberately break the law and ignore the high risk involved. Talking on a cell phone or texting messages divide your attention and make it hard to use the vehicle controls properly. By not focusing your eyes ahead, the probability of causing an accident, killing a pedestrian or a cyclist is increased by a large percentage. Even if you are using a hands-free set, the device diverts your concentration. Because they are a risk on the road, it is advisable to park at a safe location before using or answering the phone.

Things do happen very quickly on the road. In one instance, the road may be clear, in the next, there is an obstruction. It is not a place you can kill two birds with one stone.

At the same time, sparingly use your music system in your vehicle. If possible, completely refrain from listening to loud music, inserting a CD or tuning a radio while driving. You can set the radio to a station you desire before you drive away. However, do not pay full attention to the system; otherwise, you will lose concentration on the road.

## 3.0 Driving at Night

It is at night that most traffic accidents occur, especially in areas where there are no streetlights. When visibility is limited, it becomes difficult to judge the position and speed of other road users. Large trucks prefer to move at night for the reason that the roads are cool. When approaching them, reduce your speed and drive near the kerb.

Use flashlights only when they are no oncoming traffic. If you see a vehicle approaching, switch to dipped or dimmed headlights until you have gone past it. Be considerate and do not dazzle a driver who requests you to dim your headlights when he or she flashes at you.

Pedestrians and cyclists are difficult to spot at night,, especially if they are not wearing reflectors. In busy or residential areas, pedestrians cross the road behind other moving vehicles. Be on the lookout for them. Drive slowly and carefully.

## 4.0  Giving Signals

The signals often used are indicator and brake lights. The amount of time you give other road users to see you before you manoeuvre is very crucial. Signalling too early or too late can be misleading. Do it in good time to allow others to see you and respond safely. At road junctions, obtain eye contact with other road users, and make a manoeuvre only when you know that it is safe. Cancel the signal soon after you have carried out the manoeuvre.

Make use of mirrors, too, to monitor the positions of other vehicles and assess their speed and distance. Then respond correctly and in good time. One way is to adjust your speed to allow them to complete their manoeuvre. However, look out for drivers who may not cancel their indicator lights. Be cautious and do not go forward until you can ascertain that he or she has begun to slow down.

When you realise that you have missed a turn you had intended to take, avoid surprising other road users by making sudden manoeuvres. Instead, continue driving until you find a suitable place to turn back.

## 5.0  Overtaking Long Vehicles

Overtaking long vehicles is not easy because it takes longer to pass them. The longer you take to overtake, the more dangerous it becomes because the road situation is constantly changing. Oncoming traffic will be drawing closer, or you will be approaching a bend or a blow of a hill. If the vehicle you wish to overtake is moving at more than 70 Km/h, ensure the road ahead is straight and long.

Usually, drivers of large vehicles may not see you when you are right behind

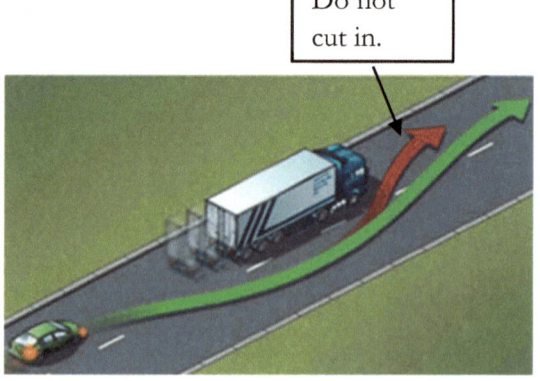

Figure 10.2- Overtake only when the road is safe.

them. Before you overtake, drop back to increase the gap between you and the large vehicle. Then edge out a little to see if the road is straight and sufficiently clear. The driver of the large vehicle will then be in a position to see you. If possible, sound your horn to alert him of your presence. Then accelerate and drive past it, leaving it plenty of room.

## 6.0   What to Do When Your Vehicle Breaks Down

A broken down vehicle is likely to obstruct other vehicles on the road. If your car develops an engine problem or a tyre puncture, get it off the road as soon as possible. Then make all passengers leave the vehicle and wait at a safe distance. Also ensure that you keep children under control. Clear the road so that traffic can continue flowing smoothly.

Next, switch on the hazard lights to warn other road users of an obstruction. In addition, place reflective warning triangles in front and behind the vehicle. If the breakdown is around a bend, or on a downhill slope, place one of the triangles before the bend or on an uphill slope so that other drivers can see it well in advance.

After placing the triangles, do not stand near the vehicle. You or a mechanic should not attend to the car in the middle of the road unless it is practically impossible to move it. Take great care because there is no guarantee that all road users will see the warning lights or triangles. Breakdowns at night pause even much more risk especially in an area where there are no streetlights. As soon as possible, call for a breakdown service to tow or repair the vehicle.

## 7.0   What to Do When an Accident Occurs

In the event that you are involved in a road accident, and someone is injured, or one or more vehicles are damaged, or an animal has been killed or injured, you should stop the vehicle and remain at the scene.

Do not drive off to escape. Even if you are not at fault, do not break into a rage and start an exchange of bad words. Instead, look for witnesses and remain calm. Immediately call an emergency number for the required service. Failing to stop and report the incident to the police is an offence. The law will treat you as a "hit-and-run" offender and prosecute you in the courts of law.

## 8.0   Observing Temporary Signs

Whenever you are approaching an area where some roadwork is going on, prepare to slow down. Make sure you observe any temporary signs maintenance staff have posted. When a mandatory speed limit sign is in place, you must

Road works

reduce your speed because of the presence of men and women carrying out these works. Slow-moving or stationary vehicles may block a traffic lane or the entire carriageway. By driving safely along that stretch of the road, you play a big role to ensure safety on the road. Your cooperation will be appreciated by everyone concerned.

# 9 BEFORE AND AFTER PASSING THE TEST

Your next step after completing all the lessons in this book is to attempt your driving test. Provided you have completed the course, you should pass it at the first attempt. You will demonstrate to the examining officer that you have the necessary skills and knowledge. He or she expects you to understand the traffic signs, road markings and drive safely.

Study the following rules in the Highway Code before you proceed with this chapter:

| Rule No. | Rule |
|---|---|
| 102, 103 | Emergency vehicles and public procession |
| 104 | Island on the road |
| 106, 230, 231 | Towing, obstructions, road works |
| 232, 233 | First Aid |

## 1.0   Taking a Mock Test

One reason learner drivers fail the test is that they become anxious to an extent they lose self-confidence. Remember that you do not have to go for the test soon after completing the course. To overcome any anxiety, let your instructor give you a mock test before you make an appointment. This will calm your nerves and give you a clue of what to expect. You are at liberty to delay and continue practising until you are ready. If you feel uncomfortable about a topic or topics in the course, you can go back and clear any uncertainties.

After passing the test, you will start driving on your own. You need to ensure that you can drive safely all the time. Remember that you have not yet gained all the necessary experience. During the time you are developing your skills, comply with the traffic regulations and respond correctly to other road users. Be alert as you drive along and anticipate other road users' behaviour to prevent any collisions.

Do not be influenced by your friends or other road users to drive faster than your normal driving speed. Furthermore, refrain from competing with other drivers. There is a temptation when someone is overtaking you to increase the speed. Be responsible for their safety and yours by keeping your speed down.

## 2.0 Routine Checks

Carrying out routine checks and regular maintenance ensure your vehicle always performs at an optimum. This includes cleaning the engine. Regular checks enable you to identify the problems in their early stages and eliminate any serious repair work. On the other hand, it becomes very expensive to wait for a break down before you decide to have it repaired. Besides, some of the worst road traffic accidents are due to worn out parts that have finally disintegrated.

As a qualified driver, you will need to understand basic components of the engine, and when the need arises, do certain simple chores. You should identify the engine oil dipstick, oil refill cap, power steering dipstick, washer liquid tank, battery,

Figure 9.1 – Engine components.

water reservoir and radiator, windscreen washer, brake fluid and fuse box.

| 1. | Brake fluid tank. | 2. | Washer liquid tank. |
|---|---|---|---|
| 3. | Engine oil filler cap | 4. | Engine oil dipstick |
| 5. | Battery. | 6. | Positive lead (colour coded) |

Under normal circumstances, your vehicle is seen by a qualified motor mechanic for a thorough service when the mileage clock has recorded a certain distance. But you can carry out simple checks on your own.

## a). Engine Oil Refill

Usually, engine oil is changed when your car is taken for a service. At times, a fuel attendant may request you to open the bonnet so he or she can check the oil level and, if necessary, top up. However, it is important that you do regular checks yourself.

Locate the engine oil dipstick as shown in figure 9.1. After pulling it out, look for markings that indicate the minimum and maximum levels. If the oil level is below minimum, top-up with oil of the same specification or grade. Be careful not to exceed the maximum level. Wipe off any spillage from the surface with a dry cloth to avoid accumulation of dust.

## b). Power Steering Oil

Without a power steering or hydraulic system, the vehicle steering would be very hard. Currently, every vehicle has this system to make the steering wheel soft to turn. A stiff steering wheel is a symptom of oil dropping below a minimum level. You will need to refill power steering oil from time to time. Check the reading on a dipstick, or container and refill with the recommended oil.

## c). Radiator and Water Reservoir

The car's cooling system should always have sufficient water in order to maintain the engine at normal temperature. If water is insufficient, the cooling system will fail to function effectively, which can cause serious problems to the engine. Ensure that the water level does not drop below the minimum level. See figure 9.2 to locate the radiator and radiator refill cap.

When the engine is running, the water in the radiator gets extremely hot. You should not open it until the engine has cooled down. To open the radiator refill cap, press and turn it anti-clockwise to let the pressure escape. Then remove the cap completely to check the level of coolant or water. If the engine is still hot, cover the cap with a thick cloth before opening it to prevent the water from scalding your hand. You can add coolant or water to bring the level to maximum.

You will need to flush the dirty water every two years.

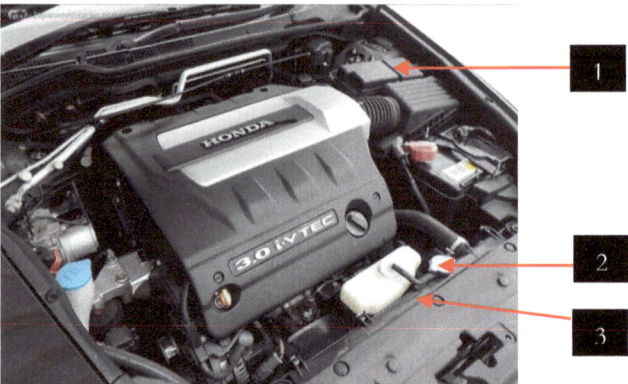

Figure 9.2 – Engine components.

1.  Fuse box.          2.   Radiator refill cap.
3.  Radiator.

### d).  Battery Maintenance

Sometimes, your vehicle can fail to start because the battery power is weak or battery acid level is below minimum. In addition, the vehicle can fail to start because battery terminals are loose. To avoid such problems, occasionally check the battery acid level and inspect the terminals.

Open each cell and, if necessary, top-up with distilled water. Remember that battery acid is harmful. Do not expose your eyes, skin or clothes to the acid. If you accidentally touch the acid, at once clean your hands with water and soap.

The positive and negative terminals (red and black respectively) sometimes accumulate corrosive substance. Use clean, hot water to remove it. Make sure the dirty water does not leak into the battery. Apply grease to stop the terminals from rusting.

### e).  Brake Fluid Reservoir

Brake fluid is a liquid used in hydraulic brakes. When the liquid is at maximum level, the brakes will operate effectively. However, if the level is below the minimum, the brakes will fail to function effectively. Moreover, if you notice that the car pulls to one side after applying the brakes, it is either the brakes are faulty or the air-pressure in the four tyres is not matching. You should have the problem rectified.

You can check the brake fluid level without removing the cap on the transparent reservoir. Refill to maximum level with approved grade. Wipe off any spillage from the surface with a dry cloth to avoid dust accumulating. Also, renew it once a year to achieve maximum performance. See figure 9.1.

## f). Windscreen Washer

Water in the windscreen washer tank is used to clean the windscreen. Check that there is enough water, mixed with window cleaning liquid. At the same time, inspect the wiper blades. If these are worn out, they will leave scratch marks on the windscreen or fail to work effectively. Remove any greasy or oily matters on the windscreen by operating the wiper-washer lever. Do not clean the windscreen with a cloth stained with oil.

## g). Tyres

Examine your tyres regularly to determine their condition. Good tyres should be free from cuts, bulges, one-sided wear, or other defects. The recommended minimum tread depth is 1.6mm. Always examine your tyres before and after going on a long journey.

If you notice any defect, replace the tyre immediately. Worn out tyres can easily puncture and will not perform well when you apply the brakes.

Tyres function better when you properly inflate them according to the manufacturer's specifications. You will find the required pressure per square inch (psi), or KPO on the side of tyres. When you inflate tyres to the correct pressure, they will have a better grip on the road and last longer. Under-inflated front tyres make the vehicle difficult to steer. On the other hand, too much air-pressure can cause the tyres to wear out or puncture easily, especially in hot weather.

Figure 9.3 – Check your tyre for defects.

It is advisable to replace the four tyres at the same time. However, if this is not possible, replace the two front, or two rear tyres at the same time. This will ensure they wear out at the same time.

After replacing them, take your vehicle for wheel alignment and balancing in order to give you good steering control and prevent them from unevenly wearing out.

### h). Shock Absorbers

Shock absorbers maintain the stability of your car as you turn at corners or drive on rough surfaces. If you notice that the car bounces more than once, then the shocks are worn out. Not only do they make it difficult to control your vehicle, but also make it easy to cause an accident or to throw you off the road. In addition, delaying to change the shocks result in other parts of your vehicle to loosen or wear out easily.

To test the condition of a shock, stand at one end of your vehicle. Then press down the front or rear of your car. A bad shock absorber will bounce twice or more. Replace all the four shocks.

### i). Spare Kit

Minor repairs do not necessarily require the attention of a qualified mechanic. You can inspect the headlights and indicator lights to ensure they are clean and operative. Look for blown out light bulbs by switching them on. Replace them with new ones.

At times, your vehicle may refuse to start due to an electrical fault. Begin by looking for blown out fuses in the fuse box. Locate a fuse map to identify the type of fuse. Each fuse differs from another in terms of voltage. Pull out the concerned fuse and inspect it carefully. Inside is a wire connecting the two copper cathodes. A faulty fuse has a snapped wire. Make sure you replace a fuse with a correct voltage.

Some of the parts to include in your spare kit are:

- A set of fuses.
- A set of light bulbs.
- A set of V-belts (fan and alternator belts).
- A set of spanners or a toolkit for minor repairs.
- A jack and wheel spanner, and
- A tyre.

### 3.0 Changing a Flat Tyre

To change a flat tyre, find a firm and level ground. Engage park for an automatic gearbox, or reverse gear for a manual gearbox.

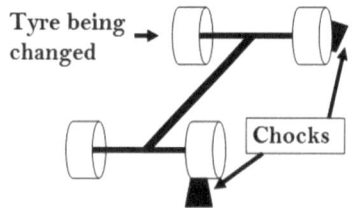

a). Apply the handbrake to lock the rear wheels.

b). Retrieve your spare wheel, a pair of chocks, a jack and wheel spanner from the boot.

Figure 9.4 – Place chokes behind the tyres.

c). Place the chocks as shown in figure 9.4.

d). Place the jack under the vehicle at a jacking point between the two grooves. See figure 9.5.

e). Remove the wheel cover and loosen the wheel nuts using a wheel spanner. Do not remove the nuts yet.

f). Raise the jack until the top of the jack touches the vehicle. Make sure it is in position.

g). Continue raising the jack until the flat tyre is raised off the ground.

h). Then, untie and remove all the wheel nuts. Remove the flat tyre.

i). Get a spare wheel and line it up with the bolts on the wheel hub.

j). First, tie the four nuts by hand. Then tighten them in a criss-cross fashion with the spanner, as shown in figure 9.6.

Figure 9.5 – Jacking point.

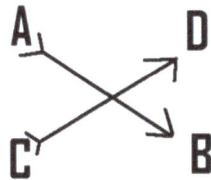

Figure 9.6 – Tighten the nuts in a sequence of A, B, C and D.

k). When you are done, lower the vehicle by turning the jack handle anti-clockwise.

l). Then remove the jack and again tighten the nuts until they are fully secured.

m). Store the flat tyre, chocks, jack and spanner in the boot.

Keep the cost of replacing tyres down by driving at between 80 and 100 km/h when you are on a long journey. When driving in excess of 120 km/h, tyres wear out very fast.

Each time you are inflating the four tyres, make sure the spare tyre is also inflated to the correct pressure.

## 4.0 Daily and Weekly Checks

If you cannot do all the checks yourself, get somebody more conversant to assist. A quick look around the vehicle is all that you need. The table below shows the frequency of inspecting each of the items:

| Table 9.1 | |
|---|---|
| **Daily and Weekly Check List** | |
| **Name** | **Frequency** |
| Fuel | Everyday |
| Headlights | Everyday |
| Indicator lights | Everyday |
| Reverse and brake lights | Everyday |
| Tyres | Everyday / each time before you go on a long journey |
| Licence plate lights | Everyday |
| Engine oil | Once a week |
| Radiator water | Once a week |
| Windscreen washer liquid | Once a week – during the rainy season |
| Brake fluid | Once a month |
| Battery | Once a week |

www.ingramcontent.com/pod-product-compliance
Lightning Source LLC
Chambersburg PA
CBHW040305010626
45792CB00025B/1049